G R I E F

31-DAY DEVOTIONALS FOR LIFE

A Series

DEEPAK REJU
Series Editor

Addictive Habits: Changing for Good, by David R. Dunham
After an Affair: Pursuing Restoration, by Michael Scott Gembola
Contentment: Seeing God's Goodness, by Megan Hill
Doubt: Trusting God's Promises, by Elyse Fitzpatrick
Grief: Walking with Jesus, by Bob Kellemen
Pornography: Fighting for Purity, by Deepak Reju

G R I E F

WALKING
WITH JESUS

BOB KELLEMEN

P&R
PUBLISHING
P.O. BOX 817 • PHILLIPSBURG • NEW JERSEY 08865-0817

Printed in the United States of America

Library of Congress Cataloging-in-Publication Data

Names: Kellemen, Robert W., author.
Title: Grief : walking with Jesus / Bob Kellemen.
Description: Phillipsburg : P&R Publishing, 2018. | Series: 31-day devotionals for life | Includes bibliographical references.
Identifiers: LCCN 2018027282| ISBN 9781629954912 (pbk.) | ISBN 9781629954929 (epub) | ISBN 9781629954936 (mobi)
Subjects: LCSH: Consolation--Meditations. | Grief--Religious aspects--Christianity--Meditations.
Classification: LCC BV4905.3 .K43 2018 | DDC 242/.4--dc23
LC record available at https://lccn.loc.gov/2018027282

Contents

Tips for Reading This Devotional

EARLY IN OUR MARRIAGE, my wife and I lived on the top floor of a town house, in a small one-bedroom apartment. Whenever it rained, leaks in the roof would drip through the ceiling and onto our floors. I remember placing buckets in different parts of the apartment and watching the water slowly drip, one drop at a time. I put large buckets out and thought, *It'll take a while to fill them.* The water built up over time, and often I was surprised at how quickly those buckets filled up, overflowing if I didn't pay close enough attention.

This devotional is just like rain filling up a bucket. It's slow, and it builds over time. Just a few verses every day. Drip. Drip. Drip. Just a few drops of Scripture daily to satiate your parched soul.

We start with Scripture. God's Word is powerful. In fact, it's the most powerful force in the entire universe.[1] It turns the hearts of kings, brings comfort to the lowly, and gives spiritual sight to the blind. It transforms lives and turns them upside down. We know that the Bible is God's very own words, so we read and study it to know God himself.

Our study of Scripture is practical. Theology should change how we live. It's crucial to connect the Word with your struggles. Often, as you read this devotional, you'll see the word *you* because Bob speaks directly to you, the reader. The readings contain a mixture of reflection questions and practical suggestions. You'll get much more from this experience if you answer the questions and do the practical exercises. Don't skip them. Do them for the sake of your own soul.

Our study of Scripture is worshipful. Grief can cast a dark cloud over your life, as truth feels cold and sadness is overwhelming. You've lost your orientation toward the One who should rule your life, and you need to turn back to him. The Word points you to Christ, who comforts you in your grief, brings hope in the midst of sadness, and charts a course through your suffering. The goal of your time in God's Word should always be worship. While the dark clouds still hover over you, Christ helps you to worship him again. The loss is painful, but the comfort and hope of your Savior is very real, as he renews your worship.

If you find this devotional helpful (and I trust that you will!), reread it in different seasons of your life. Work through it this coming month, and then come back to it a year from now, to remind yourself how Jesus brings comfort and hope in your suffering.

This devotional is *not* meant to be a comprehensive guide to coping with grief. Good volumes are already written for that purpose. Buy them and make good use of them. You'll see several resources listed at the end of the book.

That's enough for now. Let's begin.

Deepak Reju

INTRODUCTION

"Man of Sorrows"

*He was despised and rejected by men, a man of sorrows
and acquainted with grief. (Isa. 53:3)*

The Gospel and Grief

Grief. It comes in all forms and fashions, because loss comes in all shapes and sizes. When we think of grief, our souls tend to focus especially on the devastating grief that accompanies death. Yet life is filled with daily *mini*-caskets—losses great and small. A critical word. A critical accident. Betrayal, rejection, a stab in the back. The terminal diagnosis. Separation and divorce. A church split. A prodigal child. Job termination. The list, sadly, goes on and on.

The gospel. We know it has *everything* to say about grace for sin. But does the gospel have *anything* to say about grace for grief? We know that Jesus came to save sinners, but does he understand and care about our suffering?

He understands. "He was despised and rejected by men, a man of sorrows and acquainted with grief" (Isa. 53:3). Jesus intimately and intensely experienced grief, sorrow, loss, and pain.

He cares. "Surely he has borne our griefs and carried our sorrows" (Isa. 53:4). The intensity of his sympathy made him feel your grief as his own—and then do something about it. He came to crush sin, Satan, and death so that *one day* there will never again be separation, suffering, sorrow, crying, grief, or pain (see Rev. 21:4).

The author of Hebrews, who was steeped in Old Testament passages like Isaiah 53, adds his assurance of Jesus's compassion, care, and comfort and of the gospel's help, hope, and healing. "For

9

we do not have a high priest who is unable to sympathize with our weaknesses, but one who in every respect has been tempted as we are, yet without sin. Let us then with confidence draw near to the throne of grace, that we may receive mercy and find grace to help in time of need" (Heb. 4:15–16). Jesus is not only a man of sorrows; he cares about *your sorrow*. Jesus is not only acquainted with his own grief; he is acquainted with *your grief*.

A Grief Journey with Jesus

And not only is Jesus acquainted with your grief, he is always *with you* in your grief—he walks with you in the cool of the day, and *he journeys with you* in the ups and downs of your grief (see John 14:1–6; 16:33). Grief is not a series of stages that you complete in some stereotypical consecutive order. Grief is a very individual process—a personal journey that we take with our personal suffering Savior.

What Isaiah predicts and the author of Hebrews declares, the Gospels describe. From birth into a broken world, to death at the hands of a sinful world, and everywhere in between, the Gospels guide us on *a grief journey with Jesus.* The sorrows of Jesus appear on every page of the Gospels. Jesus lived, breathed, walked, and ministered in the midst of scenes of sorrow.

And the Jesus of the Gospels is not only the caring Shepherd—which brings us amazing comfort. He is also the sovereign King—which instills us with amazing confidence. "Since then we have a great high priest who has passed through the heavens, Jesus, the Son of God, let us hold fast our confession" (Heb. 4:14). We entrust ourselves to him because he sovereignly shepherds us—guiding us to the green pastures of mercy, grace, and help as we walk through our valley of the shadow of death.

When life is knocking us down, how do we hold fast? We hold fast by holding on to Jesus, who is holding us close to his heart. "He will tend his flock like a shepherd; he will gather the lambs in his arms; he will carry them in his bosom, and gently lead those that are with young" (Isa. 40:11).

In the pages that follow, we will journey together with Jesus, applying the following gospel truths to our grief journey:

- Jesus is a suffering Savior who is intimately acquainted with our grief. *It's normal to hurt.*
- Jesus is a compassionate Savior who lovingly consoles us in our grief. *It's possible to find comfort in our hurt.*
- Jesus is a healing Savior who compassionately speaks eternal truth into our earthly wounds. *It's possible to grieve with hope.*
- Jesus is an empowering Savior who mightily enables us to comfort others with the comfort we receive from God. *It's supernatural to love in the midst of loss.*

In our journey, we will grieve together . . . *and* we will hope together (see 1 Thess. 4:13).

Shared Sorrow Is
Endurable Sorrow

In the beginning was the Word, and the Word was
with God, and the Word was God. (John 1:1)

SINCE WE'RE TAKING a chronological grief journey through the life of Christ, you may expect us to begin in the beginning with baby Jesus. Instead, we're *beginning before the beginning*—in eternity past with the creator Christ.

In the beginning, the Word *was with* God. This doesn't mean that every once in a while God the Son just happened to hang out with God the Father. No—the word *was* in the Greek past tense means that Father and Son were continuously, always together in uninterrupted fellowship. And the Greek word *with* portrays face-to-face, soul-to-soul, intimate communion. If we time traveled back into eternity past, no matter when we arrived, we would find the Father, Son, and Holy Spirit in perfect, joyful relationship.

What does this possibly have to do with our grief? Jesus left all that—all that perfect, joyful, uninterrupted fellowship—in order to *reestablish relationship with us.* "And the Word became flesh and dwelt among us" (John 1:14). The eternal God pitched his tent with his finite, fallen creation.

Talk about loss! Jesus chose the loss of endless face-to-face fellowship with his Father so that he could endure the rejection of his creation. Talk about grief! "He came to his own, and his own people did not receive him" (John 1:11).

Hebrews 2:14–15, 17 explains why Jesus would endure such loss and grief: "Since therefore the children share in flesh and blood, he himself likewise partook of the same things, that through death he might destroy the one who has the power of death, that is, the devil, and deliver all those who through fear of death were subject to lifelong slavery. . . . Therefore he had to be made like his brothers in every respect, so that he might become a merciful and faithful high priest in the service of God."

Jesus did this so that he could identify with us, could destroy death and Satan, and could deliver us from the fear of death. Death is the greatest grief. Jesus left the throne of glory, was made like us in every respect, and became a merciful and faithful High Priest who cleanses us from our sins and frees us from the grip of grief.

Many years ago when I was teaching on grief, one of my parishioners shared a phrase that has stuck with me: *Shared sorrow is endurable sorrow.* We were never meant to suffer alone; we are meant to comfort and encourage one another.

John 1 and Hebrews 2 combine to teach us that. *Sorrow shared with the infinite Creator is infinitely endurable sorrow.* Jesus became flesh in order to help the frail offspring of Abraham—you and me. Jesus became flesh in order to help those who are suffering and being tempted—you and me.

Jesus became flesh so he could destroy the ultimate cause of all sorrow: sin, Satan, separation, and death.

Reflect: *Shared sorrow is endurable sorrow.* What human friends are you going to for comfort and encouragement? You were never meant to grieve alone.

Reflect: *Sorrow shared with the infinite Creator is infinitely endurable sorrow.* What would it look like, even today, for you to take your sorrow to the creator Christ—who chose to enter deeply into your grief—and seek his comfort and encouragement?

DAY 2 ✓

Entering Your Broken World

"To give light to those who sit in darkness and in the shadow of death, to guide our feet into the way of peace." (Luke 1:79)

JESUS LEFT THE throne of glory (see John 1:1–18) not for more glory, but for a broken world. He was born into a line of broken people, born to parents perceived to be immoral, born in a lowly manger, and born to a people living in darkness and the shadow of death. All our beautiful, bucolic nativity scenes belie the fact that the narrative of Christ's birth is a narrative of suffering, shame, loss, and grief.

The Bible is real and raw. The Gospels convey that reality of a fallen world from beginning to end. Matthew's genealogy of Jesus includes Abraham, who was willing to give his wife to another man in order to protect himself. It includes Judah and Tamar—a father-in-law who slept with his daughter-in-law. It includes Rahab the prostitute. It includes murderous, lustful David and the wife of his adultery. It includes Solomon—the man of seven hundred wives and three hundred concubines. Even these figures who were celebrated as heroes committed serious, shameful sins—making the reality of a fallen world all the more painfully obvious. Not even our role models can escape being tainted by shame!

Then there's the (false) shame that Joseph and Mary endured. "Her husband Joseph, being a just man and unwilling to put her to shame, resolved to divorce her quietly" (Matt. 1:19). And there's the King of Kings being born in a manger because there was no room for his family in the inn (see Luke 2:7). His lowly lineage and birth were the cause of mocking and unbelief. "Coming to his hometown he taught them in their synagogue, so that they were astonished, and said, 'Where did this man get this wisdom and these mighty works? Is not this the carpenter's son?'" (Matt. 13:54–55). Jesus was born to a nobody in Nowheresville.

Zechariah summarizes well the broken world that Jesus entered. This child, who will be called the Most High, was born among the lowliest, "to give light to those who sit in darkness and in the shadow of death" (Luke 1:79).

Daily we live in darkness—the darkness of yet another church split; the darkness of an adult child who announces that he or she has renounced the faith. Daily we walk through our own shadow of death—the shadow of pending layoffs, of a looming health crisis, of the revelation of a spouse caught with pornography . . .

But Jesus, who is the Light of the World, has entered our darkened world in order to shine on us and "to guide our feet into the way of peace" (Luke 1:79). The Bible doesn't pretend, and neither does Jesus. If you forget everything else, remember that *Jesus understands brokenness.*

The Bible never asks you to deny your loss or suppress your grief, and neither does Jesus. Remember, *it's normal to grieve.*

At the same time, the Bible never leaves us without hope, and neither does Jesus. In the midst of our suffering, Jesus offers us light (an eternal perspective on our grief and loss) and peace (shalom and wholeness in the midst of shame and despair). Remember, *it's possible to hope and heal.*

Reflect: *Jesus understands brokenness.* How does the brokenness of Jesus's world touch the brokenness of your soul?

Reflect: *It's normal to hurt and grieve.* The Bible and Jesus give you permission to grieve. What would it read like for you to express your grief over your valley of the shadow of death?

Reflect: *It's possible to hope and heal.* What would it be like for you today to receive Christ's eternal perspective and daily peace in the midst of your feelings of shame and despair?

DAY 3

Grief Sandwiched by Glory

"For my eyes have seen your salvation." (Luke 2:30)

"A sword will pierce through your own soul." (Luke 2:35)

She began to give thanks to God and to speak of him to all who were waiting for the redemption of Jerusalem. (Luke 2:38)

GRIEF IS A journey. But you and I know that it's not a straight line from one point to another. The messy, mixed-up journey of grief that zigs and zags from hills to valleys, from valleys to hills, is not a nice, neat process.

Mary and Joseph experienced this trek during the early weeks of Jesus's life. Their lives had already been turned upside down—a skeleton-in-the-closet lineage; pregnancy before marriage; a birth in a lowly manger—when they brought their child to Jerusalem to present him to the Lord.

First they encounter a holy man named Simeon. Imagine the peace they feel when Simeon speaks *glory* to them. Taking Jesus into his arms, Simeon blesses God. "Lord, now you are letting your servant depart in peace, according to your word; for my eyes have seen your salvation that you have prepared in the presence of all peoples, a light for revelation to the Gentiles, and for glory to your people Israel" (Luke 2:29–32). No wonder Mary and Joseph "marveled at what was said about him" (Luke 2:33).

But the glory was not to last long.

Now the grief: "Simeon blessed them and said to Mary his mother, 'Behold, this child is appointed for the fall and rising of many in Israel, and for a sign that is opposed (and a sword will pierce through your own soul also), so that thoughts from many hearts may be revealed'" (Luke 2:34–35).

Some blessing! I've been to and administered scores of baby dedications. Never have I heard a "blessing" like this. "Your child's life and ministry will be like a sword piercing through your soul!"

One moment they experience the sigh of relief and rest—their son is the Savior! The very next moment Mary and Joseph experience pain and agony. Mary surely remembered these words as she grieved during the crucifixion of her precious Son.

Sometimes there's hardly time to feel. Life shifts and quakes too quickly beneath our trembling feet. That was true for Mary and Joseph, as they went on to receive the second blessing—grief sandwiched by glory.

Anna, an eighty-four-year-old prophetess, had waited decade after decade for the redemption of Israel. Her wait ended in God's perfect, sovereign timing. "Coming up at that very hour she began to give thanks to God and to speak of him to all who were waiting for the redemption of Jerusalem" (Luke 2:38). Finally, redemption! After decades of waiting alone as a childless widow in worshipful fasting and praying, Anna's redemption drew near.

It's vital for us to enter grief candidly and biblically. Yet it's equally vital that we recognize that where sin and suffering abound, *grace and hope superabound*. The narrative of Simeon and Anna illustrates this biblical "sandwiching" of glory—grief—glory. We grieve not as the hopeless ones but as the ones who know the Hope of the world.

Reflect: What are some of the hills and valleys, ups and downs, of your grief journey? Where was God in your valley? Where was he in your glory—your times of hope?

Act: In our grief, it's sometimes difficult to believe that where suffering abounds, Christ's hope superabounds. Craft a prayer of hope—or at least a prayer that you would cling to Christ, who is your Hope, in the midst of your pain.

DAY 4

The Voice of Lament and
the Promise of Hope

*"A voice was heard in Ramah, weeping and loud
lamentation, Rachel weeping for her children; she refused to
be comforted, because they are no more." (Matt. 2:18)*

*"I will turn their mourning into joy; I will comfort them,
and give them gladness for sorrow." (Jer. 31:13)*

IT'S A PART of the Christmas narrative that we leave out of our
Christmas messages and Christmas cards. Enraged, Herod slew
all the male children aged two and under who were in and around
Bethlehem. Imagine the horror. The pain. The grief.

The Bible encourages us to give voice to our grief. It's called
lament. Read again the words of Matthew 2:18 above. "Because
they are no more"—what an expression of loss . . .

God gives you permission to grieve. Voice your grief.

But God, who is the God of resurrection hope, never stops at
lament. Matthew 2:18 is a quote from Jeremiah 31:15. And Jeremiah 31 pictures for us a sympathetic Shepherd who hears our
lament, acts on our voiced pain, enters our suffering, and promises his resurrection hope.

Do you feel abandoned in your grief? Hear God's shepherding promise in Jeremiah 31:10. "He who scattered Israel will
gather him, and will keep him as a shepherd keeps his flock."

Do you feel too weak to go on? Receive God's omnipotent
promise from Jeremiah 31:11. "The LORD has ransomed Jacob
and has redeemed him from hands too strong for him."

Does it seem like the darkness and despair will never lift?
Cling to God's goodness and his promise of hope. "Then shall the

young women rejoice in the dance, and the young men and the old shall be merry. I will turn their mourning into joy; I will comfort them, and give them gladness for sorrow. I will feast the soul of the priests with abundance, and my people shall be satisfied with my goodness" (Jer. 31:13–14).

The very next verse, Jeremiah 31:15, is the verse that Matthew quotes about lamentation and bitter weeping in Ramah. In the direct context of loss, God directly promises his comforting presence.

So how does our sovereign Shepherd respond to your unrelenting grief? He promises that "there is a reward for your work," that "there is hope for your future," and that you will "be restored" (Jer. 31:16, 17, 18).

Lament and hope. The apostle Paul models both in 2 Corinthians 1:8–9. "For we were so utterly burdened beyond our strength that we despaired of life itself. Indeed, we felt that we had received the sentence of death. But that was to make us rely not on ourselves but on God who raises the dead."

As you candidly lament your loss, do you *also* believe that God is *the God who raises the dead*? When you feel the sentence of death, and you despair even of life, do you *also* cling to the one who is the Resurrection and the Life?

> **Reflect:** Candid lament requires that we see God as the Father of compassion and the God of all comfort (see 2 Cor. 1:3–7). How are you currently viewing God in his relationship with you on your grief journey? How does that view compare with this view from 2 Corinthians?
>
> **Reflect:** Clinging to hope requires that we see God as the sovereign Shepherd (see Isa. 40:10–11) and the God who raises the dead (see 2 Cor. 1:8–9). How are you currently viewing God in his relationship with you? How does this view compare with the Bible's as you journey toward hope?

DAY 5

Bread for Your Hungry Soul

But he answered, "It is written, 'Man shall not live by bread alone, but by every word that comes from the mouth of God.'" (Matt. 4:4)

AT AGE THIRTY, Jesus begins his ministry—but not in the way or the place that most of us would choose to begin our life's work. "Then Jesus was led up by the Spirit into the wilderness to be tempted by the devil" (Matt. 4:1). Alone, hungry, and tempted by the devil for forty days. What a recipe for emptiness!

Imagine starting a new job, launching a new ministry, moving to a new town, or starting a new family. Now imagine the crushed expectations when no one is around, no provision is in sight, and day by day the tempter is hissing in your ears to trust yourself, because surely God can't be trusted since he allowed *all this* to happen to you!

In our crushed expectations, in our emptiness and our grief, in our hunger and our isolation, where do we turn? Jesus answers, "It is written, 'Man shall not live by bread alone, but by every word that comes from the mouth of God'" (Matt. 4:4).

What does it look like not to live by bread alone? Jesus not only teaches us this; *he models it*. Throughout the four Gospels, in the midst of temptation, loneliness, hunger, suffering, rejection, loss, and grief, Jesus lives by God alone. Let's watch and learn.

> Rising very early in the morning, while it was still dark, he departed and went out to a desolate place, and . . . prayed. (Mark 1:35)

> After he had dismissed the crowds, he went up on the mountain by himself to pray. When evening came, he was there alone. (Matt. 14:23)

After he had taken leave of them, he went up on the mountain to pray. (Mark 6:46)

Now Jesus was praying in a certain place, and when he finished, one of his disciples said to him, "Lord, teach us to pray." (Luke 11:1)

[Jesus] lifted up his eyes to heaven, and said, "Father, the hour has come; glorify your Son that the Son may glorify you." (John 17:1)

In the rhythm of his life, Jesus constantly and consistently nourished his soul through his intimate relationship with his Father. Even as he taught us during his temptation in the wilderness, so Jesus *walked the talk* every day by talking with God every second.

One of our greatest temptations in our grief is to turn inward on ourselves. Instead, God calls us to turn upward to him. When our life stinks, our perspective shrinks—and God can become an *afterthought*. Jesus models making God an *every-thought*. In the emptiness of our grief, our Father calls us to fill the hunger of our souls with the nourishment of fellowship with his infinitely fulfilling soul.

Reflect: In Jeremiah 2:13, God tells us that his "people have committed two evils: they have forsaken me, the fountain of living waters, and hewed out cisterns for themselves, broken cisterns that can hold no water." In the emptiness of your grief, what broken cistern have you been tempted to fill your soul with?

Act: In the emptiness of your grief, how could you follow the model of Jesus by filling your soul with God, the spring of living water? Why not make some time even today to go to a quiet place in order to meditate on God's Word and pray to your listening Father?

DAY 6

Light in Your Darkness

"The Spirit of the Lord is upon me, because he has anointed me to proclaim good news to the poor. He has sent me to proclaim liberty to the captives and recovering of sight to the blind, to set at liberty those who are oppressed, to proclaim the year of the Lord's favor." (Luke 4:18–19)

YESTERDAY WE LEARNED that one of our greatest temptations in grief is the lure of turning inward on ourselves instead of turning upward to God. Grief also tempts us to turn in on ourselves instead of turning outward toward others.

Anyone who has ever grieved deeply knows exactly what I mean. All we want to do is curl up in a fetal position. We can barely take care of ourselves, so don't ask us to care about someone else!

God gets it. He understands our pain. But he also wants us to understand that the prolonged fetal position is not healthy for us, not glorifying to him, and not beneficial for others. That's why the God of all comfort offers us his comfort *so that* we can *comfort others* from the overflow of his infinite comfort (see 2 Cor. 1:3–7).

But what does this have to do with our passage for today? Consider the context. The fickle crowd first "spoke well of him and marveled at the gracious words that were coming from his mouth" (Luke 4:22). It takes all of a half a dozen verses for them to turn on him. "When they heard these things, all in the synagogue were filled with wrath. And they rose up and drove him out of the town and brought him to the brow of the hill on which their town was built, so that they could throw him down the cliff" (Luke 4:28–29).

Even in grief and rejection, what is Jesus's response? Not the fetal position, but the ministry posture. Leaving Nazareth, where he had been brought up and where they now wanted to kill him, Jesus settles in Capernaum, fulfilling another prophecy of Isaiah. "The people dwelling in darkness have seen a great light, and for those dwelling in the region and shadow of death, on them a light has dawned" (Matt. 4:16).

We know that Jesus is fully God *and* fully man (see Luke 2:52). We know that he feels the pain of life deeply—he is the man of sorrows. This God-man, this fully human person, Jesus, *while* rejected by his own people, still gives light to those in darkness.

Can we give light to others *even while* we are lamenting the darkness, pain, and loss of our lives? We can if our source of light is our relationship with our heavenly Father. Jesus's identity was not fixed on what the people he grew up with thought of him. He focused his identity on what God thought of him. "And behold, a voice from heaven said, 'This is my beloved Son, with whom I am well pleased'" (Matt. 3:17).

Even while Jesus grieved the rejection of his hometown, he lived in light of his identity in his Father: a beloved and respected Son. When we live in light of God's grace relationship with us, we can give the light of grace to others—even in our grief.

> **Reflect:** When have you been tempted in your grief to turn in on yourself and remain curled up in the fetal position? We've all been there. It's okay to admit it.
>
> **Reflect:** What would it take, even in the midst of your grief, to turn outward to others? How could knowing that you are loved and respected by God-in-Christ help you to have a ministry focus today?

DAY 7

Opening the Eyes of Your Heart

*"Those who are well have no need of a physician, but those who are
sick. Go and learn what this means: 'I desire mercy, and not sacrifice.'
For I came not to call the righteous, but sinners." (Matt. 9:12–13)*

GRIEF CLOUDS OUR eyes, causing cataracts of doubt about
who God is and *who we are*. To experience hope in the midst of
grief, we must see God-in-Christ as our compassionate Soul
Physician (see Matt. 9:12–13). And we must see who we are in
Christ—we are valued as priceless (see Matt. 12:10–14).

If anyone ever had a clouded view of the character of God, it
was the Pharisees. They saw God as a begrudging Judge. To them,
the essence of God's heart was his angry desire to condemn us. If
he ever offered us grace and kindness, it was begrudgingly—as if
he resented the imposition of having to dole out his limited sup-
ply of goodness. How blasphemous!

We see their blasphemous image of God in Matthew 9:10–
11. Jesus reclines at the table with tax collectors and sinners. The
Pharisees are aghast, since in their mind God comes to offer con-
demnation not compassion.

Jesus, overhearing their false views of God, responds, "Those
who are well have no need of a physician, but those who are sick.
Go and learn what this means: 'I desire mercy, and not sacrifice.'
For I came not to call the righteous, but sinners" (Matt. 9:12–13).

How do we see God? Like the Pharisees did—as a harsh
judge? Or as a merciful, compassionate Soul Physician who cares
about and heals our sicknesses—both of the soul and of the body?

In grief, we are tempted to view God through the lens of our
loss. Christ invites us to view the Father through the lens of the
cross.

Why does Jesus care about and heal us in our suffering and loss? Because he has compassion. He also heals us because he values his children. We see this clearly in Scripture: "A man was there with a withered hand. And they asked him, 'Is it lawful to heal on the Sabbath?'—so that they might accuse him. He said to them, 'Which one of you who has a sheep, if it falls into a pit on the Sabbath, will not take hold of it and lift it out? Of how much more value is a man than a sheep! So it is lawful to do good on the Sabbath'" (Matt. 12:10–12).

Jesus, the Creator, who fearfully and wonderfully handcrafted each of us as his poem, his opus (see Eph. 2:10), declares that we are, by grace, of inestimable value *to him*. In grief, we often feel abandoned by God—alone and unloved. Jesus stretches forth his hand to take our hand in his, looks us in the eye, and says, "You are loved and valued by grace alone in Christ alone!" Christ invites us to open the eyes of our hearts to look at God and to look at ourselves through his eyes.

Reflect: What false pictures of God have you painted when you've looked at him through the lens of your loss? What biblical images of God could you paint as you view him through the lens of the cross?

Reflect: Our pain can cause us to cry out, "Abandoned!" Christ cries out, "Valued!" What could you do today to stamp "Valued in Christ" on your heart, mind, soul, and spirit?

DAY 8

Hope for the Hopeless

"Behold, my servant whom I have chosen, my beloved with whom my soul is well pleased. I will put my Spirit upon him, and he will proclaim justice to the Gentiles. . . . And in his name the Gentiles will hope." (Matt. 12:18, 21)

MANY TIMES OUR pain and grief result from our having suffered injustice—the unfair firing, the horrific abuse, the slanderous criticism. Our pain deepens when there is no sense of justice—no one righting the wrong, no one confronting the abuser, no one standing up for our reputation.

We feel alone, abandoned, unprotected. We see ourselves as an outsider, an outcast, a reject. Even typing the words hurts me, and even reading the words hurts you, I'm sure.

If no one else will stand up for us, then our temptation is to take matters into our own hands. But the Scriptures teach us that when we see *God as our Avenger*, we don't have to take vengeance. "Beloved, never avenge yourselves, but leave it to the wrath of God, for it is written, 'Vengeance is mine, I will repay, says the Lord'" (Rom. 12:19).

Did you notice how Paul starts the verse? "Beloved." We are not alone! We are not rejected. We are beloved by the Avenger who promises to repay *all* wrong.

Paul's words remind us of our passage for today, in which Matthew also includes words about being beloved: "Behold, my servant whom I have chosen, my beloved with whom my soul is well pleased" (Matt. 12:18a). In the context and culture of the day, what comes next is shocking. "I will put my Spirit upon him, and he will proclaim justice to the Gentiles. . . . And in his name the Gentiles will hope" (Matt. 12:18b, 21).

The calling of God's Beloved is to proclaim justice *to the Gentiles*? In Jesus's name *the Gentiles* will hope? In the eyes of the Jewish religious leaders, the Gentiles were outcasts and outsiders. They had no hope for God's justice and no part in God's redemptive plans—or so the Pharisees thought and taught.

In Jesus's name there is hope for the hopeless—for those suffering the grief of injustice as outsiders. When all the injustices of your life shout, "You are not loved!" God's beloved Son invites you into the love of the Trinity. When all life's unfairness shouts, "Give up hope that wrongs will ever be righted!" God's beloved Son guarantees you justice—he *will* bring victory!

Though Jesus is meek, he is not weak. "He will not quarrel or cry aloud, nor will anyone hear his voice in the streets; a bruised reed he will not break, and a smoldering wick he will not quench, until he brings justice to victory" (Matt. 12:19–20). Jesus is fierce and ferocious in protecting you, his beloved child, and in avenging the wrong done to you—until the day when he brings total and complete justice.

> **Reflect:** Let's be honest. We all have our list of top injustices done to us. What painful instances of injustices top your list? How has the lack of justice in those events wracked your soul with feelings of abandonment and tempted your spirit with desires for vengeance?
>
> **Reflect:** Let's be hopeful. What difference can it make in your soul and spirit to see God as your Avenger? Could you, even today, take your "Top Ten Acts of Injustice" and hand it over to Jesus, the Beloved, who promises you that he *will* right all the wrongs in your life by bringing victorious justice?

DAY 9

Blessed Are Those Who Mourn . . . *Now* . . .

"Blessed are those who mourn . . ." (Matt. 5:4)

"Blessed are you who weep now . . ." (Luke 6:21)

THE BIBLE IS honest about life in our fallen, broken world. Jesus is frank and direct about what happens in our souls when our fallen world falls on us. He refuses to pretend that following him eliminates mourning. He chooses a strong word for *mourn*—one that means to lament, to wail, to bewail, to be filled with overwhelming sorrow and gut-wrenching sadness.

But he doesn't stop there. In the parallel account in Luke 6:21, Jesus shares, "Blessed are you who *weep now*, for you shall laugh." The Greek word for weeping denotes loud expressions of grief, especially in mourning for loss and death. Think of the sobbing that we have all heard at funerals.

These are just two of the honest words from the Sermon on the Mount about life in our fallen world. Consider some of the others: we will be persecuted, reviled, slandered, poor, hungry, hated, excluded, spurned as evil (see Matthew 5 and Luke 6). Jesus was never "pie in the sky" "in the sweet by-and-by." Jesus gives you permission to grieve—to mourn, weep, wail, and hurt.

Those who have studied the typical response to loss have noted that denial is a common first step on our grief journey. We pretend. In our shock, we act as if nothing has happened and nothing can hurt us or penetrate our shields.

The Bible urges us to move from denial to candor—to be honest with ourselves, with each other, and with God about life in our broken world. There's a reason that there are more psalms of lament than psalms of thanksgiving. God invites his children to be brutally honest with him about our suffering and pain.

Luke's account of the Sermon on the Mount highlights the temporal nature of our losses. "Blessed are you who are hungry *now*, for you shall be satisfied. Blessed are you who weep *now*, for you shall laugh" (Luke 6:21). It's important that we honor the "nowness" of our pain. This is especially true in our ministry to our hurting brothers and sisters in Christ. We typically race in with Romans 8:28 about how God will work all things together for good. It's interesting and instructive to note that before Paul sprints to Romans 8:28, he walks through eleven verses on suffering, futility, corruption, groaning, weakness, and moaning that cannot be uttered or put into words (see Rom. 8:17–27).

Paul models the *both/and* approach to grief. *Now*, in the midst of grief, *it is normal to hurt*. We have God's permission to grieve and groan. Once we have empathized with our hurting friends, in God's timing and at their pace, *then* we can move with them on the journey of healing hope, communicating that *it's possible to hope* even in the midst of pain and loss.

Of course, neither Matthew 5:4 nor Luke 6:21 ends with mourning or weeping. God's Word never leaves us in the casket of despair. Instead, Scripture invites us to face our casket experiences honestly and then look to the God of resurrection hope. We will take that look together tomorrow.

Reflect: Has anyone ever raced you to healing hope before they sat with you and empathized with your grief? What was that like? How did their inability to grieve with you impact your ability to grieve honestly?

Act: Consider writing a lament psalm that expresses whatever grief you're experiencing today. If it would be helpful, you might want to write a personal paraphrase of Psalm 13 or Psalm 88.

DAY 10

You *Shall* Be Comforted

"Blessed are those who mourn, for they shall be comforted." (Matt. 5:4)

"Blessed are you who weep now, for you shall laugh." (Luke 6:21)

I LOVE HOW Luke begins his account of Jesus's Sermon on the Mount. "And he lifted up his eyes on his disciples . . ." (Luke 6:20). So many times the Gospels depict Jesus lifting up his eyes—on the disciples, the crowd, the fields. His gaze is a penetrating gaze. Jesus knows and understands people (see John 2:24–25). His gaze is also a compassionate gaze. Jesus feels our pain deeply, sincerely, and empathetically. As we saw yesterday, Jesus looks on you and me with honest eyes and a tender heart that is concerned with our losses and grief.

But Jesus *knows the end of the story*—so, when he peers into your life, he sees not only your current hurt but also your future joy. As Jesus looks at you today, hear him speaking eternal truth into your temporal story. "Blessed are those who mourn, for they *shall* be comforted" (Matt. 5:4). "Blessed are you who weep now, for you *shall* laugh" (Luke 6:21).

Laugh is not a giggle. *Laugh* is a belly laugh. A guffaw! It's a whole-body laugh, a body and soul laugh. It's an uncontrollable, contagious outburst of joy spilling over. It's the leaping for joy of Habakkuk 3:18.

But why laugh? How does God turn our mourning into gladness? Jesus explains. "Rejoice in that day, and leap for joy, for behold, your reward is great in heaven" (Luke 6:23). Jesus encourages us to face candidly our current earthly story *while simultaneously* ("in that day") remembering our future eternal story ("for behold, your reward is great in heaven").

Do we maintain an eternal perspective in the midst of our grief, suffering, loss, hurt, rejection, persecution, and sickness? What difference does heaven make today? What difference does our future reward make? How could it impact us today in the midst of our present mourning and weeping if we truly believed that we would be eternally comforted and joyfully laughing forevermore?

What Jesus teaches, the apostle Paul lives. "[In Asia] we were so utterly burdened beyond our strength that we despaired of life itself. Indeed, we felt that we had received the sentence of death. But that was to make us rely not on ourselves but on God who raises the dead" (2 Cor. 1:8–9).

Paul did not pretend. He faced life honestly—he despaired of life and felt the sentence of death. But neither did Paul pretend that life ends with this life! Paul not only faced his casket experiences; he invited the resurrecting God into his casket so he could experience future hope today.

Because of the resurrecting God, in that future day, the meek *shall* inherit the earth, the hungry *shall* be satisfied, the merciful *shall* receive mercy, and the pure in heart *shall* see God. Jesus calls you to view your mourning and weeping through the lens of the future, when your God of resurrection hope will turn all your weeping into eternal glee.

Reflect: You will be eternally comforted and you will belly laugh forever. How can this future reality impact you today in the midst of your present mourning and weeping?

Reflect: Paul was skilled at facing his casket experiences while simultaneously celebrating the empty tomb—skilled at facing death while clinging to the Resurrection and the Life. What would it look like today for you to cling to your resurrecting God even while you feel the sentence of death?

DAY 11

A Portrait of Gospel
Grief with Grace

*"But I say to you who hear, Love your enemies, do good
to those who hate you, bless those who curse you, pray
for those who abuse you." (Luke 6:27–28)*

"Be merciful, even as your Father is merciful." (Luke 6:36)

WE'VE TALKED A lot about honesty in our first ten days together. Let's get honest about the passages we are pondering for today. "Kellemen, I liked what you had to say about Jesus as a suffering Savior who is acquainted with my grief. I appreciated your thoughts on Jesus as a compassionate Savior who consoles me in my pain. I enjoyed your reflections about Jesus as a healing Savior who gives me hope in my time of loss. But this stuff about Jesus as an empowering Savior who grants me strength *to love in the midst of my loss*? That's not what I expected in a devotional on grief!"

Maybe you're not thinking that, but I know I was as I combed through the four Gospels for biblical principles on grieving. Time after time, Jesus refused to stop at comforting hope. He kept pushing me not only toward comforting others, not only toward loving others, but toward forgiving and loving those who caused my grief! Consistently, directly in the context of grief and loss, Jesus gazed on my soul and through his Word said, "Bob, 'love your enemies, do good to those who hate you, bless those who curse you, pray for those who abuse you' (Luke 6:27–28)." Remember, these verses come *just five verses* after Jesus tells us, "Blessed are you who weep now, for you shall laugh" (Luke 6:21). In *the context of mourning and weeping,* Jesus calls us to a life of *forgiving and loving.* That's costly discipleship.

Though it's almost impossible to imagine in the early stages, here's God's goal for our grief: in light of our future perspective ("you shall laugh"), even while being hated, cursed, and abused, we are to do good to those who hate us, bless those who curse us, and pray for those who abuse us.[1]

How is this possible? We love like this through the power of the Spirit, by the work of the Son, and by following *the example of the Father*. When we love those who have grieved us, we are "sons of the Most High, for he is kind to the ungrateful and the evil. Be merciful, even as your Father is merciful" (Luke 6:35–36).

Jesus is not asking us to do anything that he did not do. Of those crucifying him, Jesus cried out, "Father, forgive them!" The father ran to his prodigal son—the son who had broken his heart—threw his arms around him, and celebrated his return home. Gospel grief with grace involves loving like the Trinity loves.

Recall that Romans 8:17–29 occurs in the context of suffering. What's the pinnacle, the end game, the ultimate goal of that suffering? "For those whom he foreknew he also predestined to be *conformed to the image of his Son*" (Rom. 8:29). What does healing from suffering look like? It not only looks like receiving comfort from the God of all comfort; it also looks like giving mercy like the Father of all mercy.

Reflect: Who has hurt you? Who has been a human cause of your grief and suffering? What prayer of lament do you want to cry out to God regarding this person?

Reflect: What enemy does God want you to love? What would biblical *holy love* toward that enemy look like? What prayer is God calling you to pray for someone who has hurt, harmed, or abused you?

DAY 12

Jesus Is on the Move!

As he drew near to the gate of the town, behold, a man who had died
was being carried out, the only son of his mother, and she was a widow,
and a considerable crowd from the town was with her. And when
the Lord saw her, he had compassion on her. (Luke 7:12–13)

PICTURE IT. THE Creator of life approaches the gate of the
city of Nain. "Behold, a man who had died was being carried
out" (Luke 7:12). This is not the way things were supposed to be.
Death is an intruder. An invader. But the Creator is on the move
and is about to launch his counterassault. Keep watching.

This dead man was "the only son of his mother." Literally he
was her "only begotten son." Jesus could relate! Not only is she
childless, she is also husbandless, "a widow." No wonder Luke
informs us that "when the Lord saw her, he had compassion on
her" (Luke 7:13).

Dr. Luke chooses a word for compassion that comes from the
world of anatomy and physiology. It denotes the inward parts—
"bowels of compassion." Imagine feeling something so deeply
that your stomach is in turmoil. It's a picture of the total person
at the deepest level experiencing compassion flowing from the
body, soul, spirit, heart, mind, will, affections, and emotions. The
Gospel writers use it of Jesus over a dozen times.

If you forget everything else, remember this. When you're
hurting, Jesus has infinite, passionate, unmatched compassion on
you. It's a compassion that motivates intervention.

Get ready. God is about to act. "He came up and touched the
bier [coffin], and the bearers stood still. And he said, 'Young man,
I say to you, arise.' And the dead man sat up and began to speak,
and Jesus gave him to his mother. Fear seized them all, and they

glorified God, saying, 'A great prophet has arisen among us!' and 'God has visited his people!'" (Luke 7:14–16).

Picture it again. Moved with compassion, Jesus approaches the coffin and touches it. Everyone is speechless and motionless—like an army of dead people. Just as with Lazarus, Jesus commands the young man to "Arise! Come forth!" Let what happens next sink in. A dead man sits up. A dead son speaks.

In the Greek, Luke says that Jesus gave this only begotten son *back* to his mother. What was lost is now found. What was dead is now returned.

Sometimes in this life dead things are resurrected. The persecutor apologizes. The prodigal returns home. The abuser turns himself in and begs for forgiveness. Other times, what is lost is not restored this side of heaven; but we have the promise that one day all tears, sorrow, crying, mourning, and grief will be washed away and that what was lost and dead will be returned back and made alive again.

We can be sure that one day things will be set right because the Creator has visited his people. Again, the Greek is significant. *Visited* is literally "cared for." God has cared for his people by visiting them—by being incarnated with us. When an all-compassionate and all-powerful Creator visits us, everything starts changing. It is like spring finally returning to Narnia. Every resurrection in the Gospels is a foretaste—a promissory note that Jesus is on the move!

Reflect: Carry this truth with you today: when you're hurting, Jesus has infinite, passionate, unmatched compassion for you.

Reflect: Jesus is on the move. Spring has sprung! How could you allow hope to take seed and begin to blossom in your heart today?

DAY 13

Talitha Cumi!

Taking her by the hand he said to her, "Talitha cumi," which means, "Little girl, I say to you, arise." And immediately the girl got up and began walking . . . and they were immediately overcome with amazement. (Mark 5:41–42)

A DAUGHTER DIES. "Friends" provide counsel like Job's counselors did. "Don't trouble God with your grief, Jairus! Your daughter is dead. It's too late" (see Mark 5:35). Giving up hope is a common, yet sad, response to loss.

Do we see ourselves in this response? Perhaps life has beaten us down so much and so frequently that we're like the barren Shunammite woman of 2 Kings 4, who tells Elisha, "Didn't I tell you, 'Don't raise my hopes'?" (2 Kings 4:28 NIV). Sometimes we're so embittered by life that we can't hope with those who hope. Instead, we discourage others from any glimmer of positive expectation.

Jesus offers other counsel. "Do not fear, only believe" (Mark 5:36). Fear is another common response to loss—a response best countered by belief in God's affectionate sovereignty.

Which of these responses tends to typify us—fear or belief? Jesus exhorts Jairus not to fear any longer. Given the circumstances, fear seems like a normal human response. When he last saw his little girl, she was at the point of death. Do we fear the worst and believe the least? Or do we believe the best about God and his compassionate care?

Entering the house of the ruler of the synagogue, Jesus witnesses another common response to grief. "Jesus saw a commotion, people weeping and wailing loudly" (Mark 5:38). Not knowing their hearts, we can't discern whether this was grief without hope or grief with hope. But it was surely grief.

Which type of grief characterizes our response to loss? Is it deep grief with great hope in God, or is it hopeless grief?

There are also various potential responses to God's offer of hope. "When he had entered, he said to them, 'Why are you making a commotion and weeping? The child is not dead but sleeping.' And they laughed at him" (Mark 5:39–40). They laugh. This is not the belly laugh of joy from the Sermon on the Mount. This is the derisive laugh of contempt arising from unbelief. Do we see ourselves in this response of not just hopelessness but contempt for God born out of doubt about the goodness of his heart?

We see a second response after they witness hope fulfilled. "Taking her by the hand he said to her, 'Talitha cumi,' which means, 'Little girl, I say to you, arise.' And immediately the girl got up and began walking . . . and they were immediately overcome with amazement" (Mark 5:41–42). The KJV says, "They were astonished with a great astonishment!" The Greek word gives us our word *ecstasy*, which describes a person being thrown into a state of shock and awe. The idea is to believe what is beyond belief.

Do we see ourselves in this response? Do we believe in the supernatural power of God even when everything in the natural world cries out against such belief?

Reflect: Which response to loss is typical in your life? Giving up hope? Fear? Belief? Grief with hope? Hopeless grief? How could you move toward those responses that are most God honoring? What should you do with those responses that are not honoring to God?

Reflect: When Jesus offers you hope, do you respond with contempt that doubts God's good heart, or do you respond with astonishment that believes the unbelievable because you trust God's good heart?

DAY 14

Sheep with a Shepherd

Jesus went throughout all the cities and villages, teaching in their synagogues and proclaiming the gospel of the kingdom and healing every disease and every affliction. When he saw the crowds, he had compassion for them, because they were harassed and helpless, like sheep without a shepherd. (Matt. 9:35–36)

MY OLDER BROTHER had just passed away after a five-month battle with cancer. As the family gathered around his hospice bed, I opened my Bible, preparing to read Psalm 23. Just then, the chaplain entered the room, expressed his condolences, and read Psalm 23. Soon after he left, our counseling pastor entered the room, wept with us, and read Psalm 23. Moments after he left, our senior pastor entered the room, empathized with us, and read Psalm 23.

Is any passage more frequently read during times of grief than Psalm 23? Grief and loss, suffering and pain—they make us feel like sheep without a shepherd. When we are walking through the valley of the shadow of death, we long for the assuring, comforting words: "The LORD is my shepherd; I shall not want" (Ps. 23:1).

In Matthew 9, Jesus has (1) healed a paralyzed man, (2) called an outcast tax collector to follow him, (3) raised Jairus's daughter, (4) healed the woman who touched the hem of his garment, (5) healed two blind men, and (6) healed a demon-possessed man. In this context we read, "Jesus went throughout all the cities and villages, teaching in their synagogues and *proclaiming the gospel of the kingdom and healing every disease and every affliction*" (Matt. 9:35). There is a core connection between the gospel and healing. Jesus's healing miracles were to authenticate him as the promised Messiah. But it's more than that. In the gospel, the

Creator-King invades his own kingdom to restore everything to the way it was meant to be—restoring shalom, peace, wholeness, health, and holiness.

Compare the incident in Matthew 10 with Luke 9.

> And he called to him his twelve disciples and gave them authority over unclean spirits, to cast them out, and *to heal every disease and every affliction.* (Matt. 10:1)

> And he called the twelve together and gave them power and authority over all demons and *to cure diseases,* and he sent them out *to proclaim the kingdom of God and to heal.* (Luke 9:1–2)

When the Shepherd-King comes, the sick sheep are healed. Ultimately, on that final day, everything is healed. Today, healing is sometimes physical or circumstantial, but it can always be spiritual—the healing of our hearts as we cling to our Shepherd-King.

Jesus enters our lives and our hurts—not as an aloof king who rules from afar, but as a tender, caring, compassionate Shepherd-King. "When he saw the crowds, *he had compassion for them,* because they were *harassed and helpless, like sheep without a shepherd*" (Matt. 9:36). There is a core connection between the gospel and Jesus's compassion on the hurting and suffering. Are you feeling harassed and helpless today? Run to your compassionate Shepherd-King. You are *not* a sheep without a Shepherd!

Reflect: In your grief, Satan whispers, "You are all alone! A sheep without a shepherd!" Counter his lies by meditating on Matthew 9:35–36 and the truth that Jesus is your compassionate Shepherd-King.

Reflect: How can the words of Psalm 23:1 comfort you today? "The LORD is my shepherd; I shall not want."

Act: Write your own paraphrased version of Psalm 23:1–6.

DAY 15

The Greatest Loss

While they were gathering together in Galilee, Jesus said to them,
"The Son of Man is going to be delivered into the hands of men;
and they will kill Him, and He will be raised on the third day."
And they were deeply grieved. (Matt. 17:22–23 NASB)

WHEN MARTIN LUTHER ministered to grieving Christians, he helped them to consider two "levels" of suffering. The first level involves what happens *to* us—life's painful losses and crosses. In Level 1 suffering, *the world is fallen and it often falls on us.*

As bad as that is, the second level of suffering is worse. It involves what happens *in* us—the temptation to doubt the goodness of God, the temptation to lose hope because we lose sight of who God is in Christ. The greatest loss of all is the loss of spiritual eyesight, leading to loss of faith in God's good heart. In Level 2 suffering, *the world is a mess and it messes with our minds.*

To prepare his disciples, Jesus predicted his death and resurrection on numerous occasions.[1] In response, the disciples experienced both levels of suffering. Our reading for today notes their Level 1 response: "They were deeply grieved" (v. 23 NASB). Christ's shocking news of his pending crucifixion caused their hearts to be troubled and their souls to be deeply grieved. None of us would have responded any differently.

But their response did not stop there. Consider Matthew's account of their second level of suffering: "Jesus began to show his disciples that he must go to Jerusalem and suffer many things . . . and be killed, and on the third day be raised. And Peter took him aside and began to rebuke him, saying, 'Far be it from you, Lord! This shall never happen to you.' But he turned and said to Peter, 'Get behind me, Satan! You are a hindrance to me. For you are not setting your mind on the things of God, but on the things of man'" (Matt. 16:21–23).

Think about this. Peter *rebukes Christ!* While calling him "Lord," Peter treats Christ like his servant: "Far be it from you. . . . This shall never happen to you." In his grief, Peter loses sight of who he's talking to.

Jesus, the ultimate Soul Physician, diagnoses Peter's spiritual blindness and its ultimate source. Peter loses sight of the truth that Jesus is a *suffering Savior*, sent by the Father to die for our sins. But he also loses sight of the truth that Jesus is a *healing Savior*, an *empowering Savior*, and a *victorious Savior*.

Peter's grief over Jesus's crucifixion *blinds him to the glory of Christ's resurrection!* When Peter tells Jesus that *this* shall never happen to him, *Christ's resurrection* is part of what he claims won't happen!

Before we jump on the Peter-bashing wagon, let's be honest with ourselves. Our grief can easily blind us to God's glory. Our losses can easily cause us to lose sight of Christ's resurrection power.

Reflect: Like Peter, when have you been guilty of losing sight of Christ's resurrection power?

Reflect: What "Level 1 suffering" are you grieving over today? In what ways is Satan tempting you toward "Level 2 suffering"—losing sight of God's good heart and Christ's resurrection power?

Reflect: How could keeping sight of the words "and He will be raised on the third day" enlighten your path today?

DAY 16

Life Abundant

"The thief comes only to steal and kill and destroy. I came that they may have life and have it abundantly. I am the good shepherd. The good shepherd lays down his life for the sheep." (John 10:10–11)

WE'RE AT THE halfway point of our journey together. We've talked a lot about the earthly story of pain and suffering, how *it's normal to hurt*, and how God gives us permission to grieve. We've also talked about the eternal story of healing and peace, how *it's possible to hope*, and how Christ promises us future victory.

Consider today's passage a halftime speech from the ultimate coach—Christ—in which he explains how the eternal story is meant to invade and impact our earthly story. Here's my paraphrase of Christ's halftime pep talk from John 10: "Future hope is an amazing blessing of your Christian faith. But never forget that *future hope has present results*—abundant life *today*. This hope is not some pie-in-the-sky, just-pretend-all-is-well sentimentality. No. This hope exists in the midst of ultimate reality—our fallen, broken world and the Father's promise that one day all will be well. In light of that *coming* day, even in the throes of your great grief, you can experience abundant life *today*."

You might be thinking, *Bob, if you knew what I was going through and feeling, you'd never talk to me about* abundant *living!* I hope I've made it clear by now that I do get that. Life is hard. You need someone to climb into your casket of despair and empathize with you. But I hope that you get something, too—if others and I leave you in your casket without inviting you into the daily experience of Christ's resurrection hope, then we are very poor spiritual friends.

Jesus's teaching about abundant life in John 10 is sandwiched between suffering in John 9 (a man born blind) and death in John 11 (Lazarus). Even in John 10:10 we see this mixture of death and abundant life: "The thief comes only to steal and kill and destroy. I came that they may have life and have it abundantly." Yet it's exactly in this messy context that Jesus seeks to encourage (to put courage into) his disciples with the promise of *abundant life today*.

What is this "abundant life"? The Greek word means "to have a surplus of, to overflow, to spoil." Think about that. Jesus wants to spoil you with blessings—today. Obviously, given the context of blindness and death, this is not some health-and-wealth prosperity gospel. Jesus wants to spoil you—in the midst of your grief—with the internal spiritual blessings of joy, peace, hope, faith, and love.

John 10 shows us some of those spiritual blessings. Jesus, the Good Shepherd, calls you by name, leads you with wisdom, saves you, shepherds you to green pastures, lays down his life for you, cares for you, protects you, knows you intimately, guides you with his voice, gives you perfectly secure eternal life. John 11–16 shares additional spiritual blessings of a Savior who weeps with you (John 11), gives you light in your darkness (John 12), serves you (John 13), calms your troubled hearts, does not leave you an orphan but sends his Spirit to dwell within you (John 14–15), and overcomes the world and gives you his peace (John 16). That's the abundant spiritual life that you can name and claim today.

Reflect: Future hope has present results—abundant life today. How could this one sentence impact your mindset today?

Reflect: Which of the blessings listed above from John 10–16 do you want to "name and claim" today? How could you do that?

DAY 17

The Father's Purpose

Now Jesus loved Martha and her sister and Lazarus. So, when he heard that Lazarus was ill, he stayed two days longer in the place where he was. (John 11:5–6)

Then Jesus told them plainly, "Lazarus has died, and for your sake I am glad that I was not there, so that you may believe. But let us go to him." (John 11:14–15)

"WHY?" IT'S THE haunting one-word question that we all ask when struck by loss. In one of the most compelling passages on grief and the gospel—John 11 and the story of Lazarus—Jesus tells us exactly why God allows loss. "So that you may believe" (John 11:15).

Here's what we would like to read: "Now Jesus loved Martha and her sister and Lazarus. Because he loved them, when he heard that Lazarus was ill, he miraculously transported himself to their home and healed Lazarus."

Instead, Jesus informs his disciples that Lazarus has "fallen asleep" (v. 11). He meant death; they took it to mean that Lazarus was taking a nap! Jesus now avoids all euphemisms and plainly tells them, "Lazarus has died." What he says next is confusing. "And for your sake I am glad that I was not there."

The disciples must have been astonished. "What? You're glad that you weren't there to save Lazarus? You're glad that he was allowed to die? You're glad that we're grieving and Lazarus's sisters are devastated? I thought that you hated death and came to bring life. How is it for anyone's sake and anyone's benefit that death wins?"

Jesus provides a five-word answer: *"So that you may believe."* His answer reminds us of a passage we discussed in days 4 and

10—2 Corinthians 1:8–9. Remember? Paul felt the sentence of death; he despaired of life. Why did God allow this in Paul's life? *So that* he might rely not on himself but on the God who raises the dead.

Why did God allow trouble in Paul's situation and soul? Why did God allow Lazarus to die? Because he knows what is best for us. And because he knows what is worst for us—believing in ourselves and depending on our own power and strength.

Death brings us to the end of ourselves. It shows us how finite and needy we are. Death is God's medicine of choice to crush our self-reliance.

That's why Jesus, when he heard that Lazarus was ill, stayed away two days longer. The most loving thing he could do to minister to his disciples, to Mary, Martha, and Lazarus, and to us was *to let Lazarus die.* They needed to come to the end of their rope so that they would cling to Christ alone as their rope of hope. Just like you and I need to hit rock bottom so that we will cling to the Rock of Ages.

Reflect: In what ways are you fighting against coming to the end of your rope? What would it look like for you to give up your self-reliance and to cling to Christ's rope of hope and turn to the Rock of Ages?

Reflect: Take a look back at your losses. With 20/20 spiritual hindsight, how was your loss actually for your ultimate spiritual benefit? With eyes of faith, what evidence do you see that Jesus allowed your loss *because he loves you* and knows what is best for you?

DAY 18

The Son's Passion

Jesus wept. (John 11:35)

"Jesus wept." Scripture's shortest verse contains perhaps its most often quoted words about grief. Theologians have expended thousands of words exegeting these two words. But sometimes we make this passage and Jesus's weeping more complicated than John does.

John fills the entire passage with passion and compassion that arise from personal, relational, and intimate love. He introduces us to a family—three times in the first three verses we read about a *sister*, a *brother*, and two *sisters*. John reminds us of Mary's tender anointing of Jesus and her wiping his feet with her hair. In John 11:3, the sisters highlight the closeness of Jesus's relationship with their family, saying, "Lord, *he whom you love* is ill." John captures that affection with these tender words: "Now Jesus loved Martha and her sister and Lazarus" (v. 5).

John also imbues the text with candid words of grief. Many friends come to Martha and Mary "to console them concerning their brother" (v. 19). Others are with Mary in her house "consoling her" (v. 31). When she rises, they assume she is "going to the tomb to weep" (v. 31). The mourning crescendos when Mary falls at Jesus's feet, saying, "Lord, if you had been here, my brother would not have died" (v. 32). At that moment we read some of the most tender words ever written. "When Jesus *saw her weeping*, and the Jews who had come with her *also weeping*, he was *deeply moved* in his spirit and *greatly troubled*. And he said, 'Where have you laid him?' They said to him, 'Lord, come and see.' *Jesus wept*. So the Jews said, 'See how *he loved him!*'" (vv. 33–36).

We can argue that Jesus wept because he was mourning all

death, but that seems to miss the point that John, the beloved disciple, clearly wants to make. Jesus loved *this* family. And Jesus wept with *this* family in *their* grief and *his* grief. This is sheer human sympathy and empathy for them. And it is sheer and sinless human grief. Jesus is deeply moved, groaning in his spirit—personally acquainted with grief. Truly, it's normal to hurt and it's human to grieve.

Because Christ is the God-man, his love is infinite and intimate. So you can legitimately apply John 11 to your life. When you are hurting, others could speak John 11:3 of you: "Lord, she whom you love is grieving and suffering." "Lord, he whom you love is struggling and heartbroken." In your grief, you can fill in this blank from John 11:5 with your name: "Now Jesus loves _____."

When you are weeping, know that Jesus is deeply moved in his spirit and greatly troubled. When you weep, Jesus weeps. Others can say of you in your loss, "See how Jesus loves her." "See how Jesus loves him."

Jesus wept. He wept for Lazarus, Martha, and Mary.

Jesus weeps. He weeps for you. He weeps with you.

Reflect: What would it look like for you to apply John 11:33–36 to your life?

Reflect: On earlier days in this devotional, we've shared the truth that *shared sorrow is endurable sorrow*. How does knowing that Jesus shares in your sorrow empower you to endure your sorrow?

DAY 19

The Spirit's Power

When He had said these things, He cried out with a loud voice, "Lazarus, come forth." He who had died came forth, bound hand and foot with wrappings; and his face was wrapped around with a cloth. Jesus said to them, "Unbind him, and let him go." (John 11:43–44 NASB)

THIS TEXT IS so alive with death. "Then Jesus, deeply moved again, came to the tomb. It was a cave, and a stone lay against it. Jesus said, 'Take away the stone.' Martha, the sister of the dead man, said to him, 'Lord, by this time there will be an odor, for he has been dead four days'" (John 11:38–39). Talk about the Bible being real and raw!

Into death, Jesus speaks forth life. "Lazarus, come forth" (John 11:43 NASB). Ah! The words we long for in every casket experience.

Many times in our grief, whether it's over the loss of a loved one, the loss of our own health, the loss of a significant relationship, or the loss of a job, we feel as if *we have died.* At the very least, a part of us feels dead and lost forever. That's when we want to experience resurrection power. "The man or woman who had died came forth!"

Many times, even when we experience some level of healing hope, we are much like Lazarus—a dead man walking. We feel bound hand and foot from head to toe. And we long to hear Jesus say to us, "Unbind him, and let him go!" "Loose her, and set her free!"

Sometimes our hurt is so deep that our number one goal (as well as goals two to ninety-nine) is to stop hurting. This text suggests another goal: *God's glory.* Coming alive, being set free, being unbound, finding hope—these are all wonderful results of Christ's comforting and healing ministry. But gospel-centered grief and growth is not all about us. It's all about *him*.

Jesus makes this plain from the very beginning of this narrative. "But when Jesus heard it he said, 'This illness does not lead to death. It is for the glory of God, so that the Son of God may be glorified through it'" (John 11:4). In case our grief caused us to miss it the first time, Jesus repeats the ultimate purpose of our grief journey: "Jesus said to her, 'Did I not tell you that if you believed you would see the glory of God?'" (John 11:40).

Yes, it is biblical to ask, How can I find Christ's comfort in my grief? But let's not stop there. Let's also be asking, How can I glorify the Father as I seek Christ's comfort and encouragement in my grief journey?

Reflect: How is Jesus saying to you in your grief, "The man or woman who has died, come forth"? How is Jesus saying to you, "Unbind him, and let him go"? Or, "Loose her, and set her free"?

Reflect: Seek biblical answers to two grief questions today: (1) How can I find Christ's comfort in my grief? and (2) How can I glorify the Father as I seek Christ's comfort and encouragement in my grief journey?

DAY 20

"Lord, Have Mercy"

And behold, there were two blind men sitting by the roadside,
and when they heard that Jesus was passing by, they cried out,
"Lord, have mercy on us, Son of David!" (Matt. 20:30)

I LOVE THE literary beauty of Scripture. Consider the irony of Matthew's opening phrase: "And *behold.*" This is an exclamation to *see*, to take notice, to *look on carefully.* The irony? Two blind men behold! They see spiritually while being blind physically. They use their hearing rather than their sight. They *hear* that Jesus is passing by.

During times of loss, we have to use the spiritual sense of hearing God's eternal Word and applying it to our temporal grief. Gospel-centered healing in grief requires scriptural irony—seeing the larger redemptive story with spiritual eyes even while we are surrounded by the painful loss-and-suffering story that seeks to blind us to God's good heart.

Matthew's literary artistry paints a picture not only of blind men who see but also of seeing men who are spiritually blind. The blind cry out for mercy, but the spiritually blind crowd cries something different. "The crowd rebuked them, telling them to be silent" (Matt. 20:31).

How many of us, in our grief, have been silenced? "Get over it. Don't you know that time heals all wounds? You've had more than enough time!" Those are lies of the blind. Time does not heal. The Timeless One heals.

These two blind men understand this. Which is why "they cried out all the more, 'Lord, have mercy on us, Son of David!'" (Matt. 20:31). To have *mercy* means more than feeling sympathy for another. It involves manifesting this sympathy in action.

Healing from grief requires persistent pleading. It requires resilient trust that God hears our cry for mercy and acts on our plea for help.

When people try to silence your grief, *cry out all the more* . . . to Jesus. Cry out to the "Son of David." This is a Messianic term. These two blind men beheld and recognized what the crowd was blind to—Jesus is the promised Messiah, and healing comes only through him.

Grief must have a voice. And Jesus responds compassionately to voiced grief. "Stopping, Jesus called them and said, 'What do you want me to do for you?' They said to him, 'Lord, let our eyes be opened.' And Jesus in pity touched their eyes, and immediately they recovered their sight and followed him" (Matt. 20:32–34).

In his caring counsel, Jesus asks these men a penetrating question that he would ask of us as well. "What do you want me to do for you?" They answer candidly, and Jesus responds compassionately. He feels deeply from the heart and responds actively to heal, help, and provide hope.

Matthew ends his narrative as beautifully as he began it. The men recovered their sight and followed him. But they had been following him even before they recovered their sight. They had trusted him even before they were healed. Do we? Do we follow only after the answered prayer? Or do we follow even when God seems silent?

> **Reflect:** In your grief, how do you *specifically* answer this question from Jesus: "What do you want me to do for you?"
>
> **Reflect:** Grief seeks to blind you to God's good heart. How can seeing Jesus as the Messiah—the Son of David—help you?
>
> **Reflect:** Healing requires persistent pleading and resilient trust. What is your persistent prayer to Jesus in the midst of your grief?

DAY 21

"What Shall I Say?"

"Now is my soul troubled. And what shall I say? 'Father, save me from this hour'? But for this purpose I have come to this hour. Father, glorify your name." (John 12:27–28)

IN GETHSEMANE, JESUS honestly asks that the cup be taken from him. Yet, in eternal commitment to his Father, he surrenders his will to the Father's will. "Not as I will, but as you will" (Matt. 26:39).

We often read about Jesus's turmoil in Gethsemane, think about it, and hear it preached. Yet Jesus's words here in John 12 are perhaps even more powerful, if that is possible. Having shared that he must soon die, Jesus informs us that his soul is "troubled," meaning that it is thrown into great agitation. This is perfectly understandable to anyone who has received news of an incurable illness or of pending death. Our world is turned upside down and our soul is turned inside out. *Now what?*

In yesterday's reading, two blind men cried out for mercy and asked for healing. There's nothing wrong with that. Jesus has that same option. He even specifically identifies it: "What shall I say? 'Father, save me from this hour'?"

But Jesus identifies the deeper soul issue. Do we make our requests out of self-preservation or God-glorification?

Listen to how Jesus wrestles with ultimate purpose in the face of pending death. "But for this purpose I have come to this hour. Father, glorify your name." Jesus-like grief is honest about our desire to be saved from loss. Yet it remains committed to our ultimate desire to glorify God regardless of loss or gain. The Lord giveth, and the Lord taketh away. Blessed be the name of the Lord (see Job 1:21).

It has been said that grief, loss, and suffering reveal our true god/God. All too often, when we lose something, we come to discover that what we lost was in reality a false god we had been worshipping as an idol of our hearts. We've said it a dozen times; let's say it at least once more. There is nothing wrong with grieving our loss deeply. There is something deeply wrong with prioritizing relief from pain and changed circumstances *over* glorifying God.

Jesus models doing both: grieving loss while glorifying God, feeling our pain while surrendering to our Father. What shall *you and I* say in our pain? "Save me from this"? Or "Father, glorify your name"?

Grief and loss are often so disorienting that we feel as if our purpose has been robbed from us. But what if our purpose revolves around how we handle our pain? What if our affectionately sovereign God fearfully and wonderfully made us, and wisely and caringly directed our circumstances, exactly for such a time as this and for such a purpose as showing an onlooking world what it means to trust through tragedy?

> **Reflect:** Let's each ask the question again: what shall *I* say in my pain? "Save me from this"? Or "Father, glorify your name"?
>
> **Reflect:** Have you considered that part of your eternal purpose is showing an onlooking world what it means to trust through tragedy? What would it look like this week for you to glorify God by surrendering to him and trusting your Father's good heart?

DAY 22

Jesus Laments

*"O Jerusalem, Jerusalem, the city that kills the prophets
and stones those who are sent to it! How often would I have
gathered your children together as a hen gathers her brood
under her wings, and you were not willing!" (Luke 13:34)*

WE THINK OF psalms of lament, but we don't often ponder Jesus's lament. In Luke 13, Luke 19, and Matthew 23, Jesus
laments over Jerusalem. Like a parent lamenting over a prodigal
child, so Jesus laments over prodigal Israel. Everyone with a lost
loved one can identify with Jesus's weeping lament and his con-
tinual ministry to his wayward children.

Luke 13:33 sets the very personal context for Jesus's lament.
"Nevertheless, I must go on my way today and tomorrow and the
day following, for it cannot be that a prophet should perish away
from Jerusalem." It's not just some *other* prophets that wicked,
prodigal Jerusalem kills. Jesus is to be chief among the prophets
slain in Jerusalem.

Yet he still laments *over them*—over those who will kill him!
This is hard beyond imagination. Think about that person who
has most deeply hurt you. Maybe it's the boss who unjustly fired
you. Perhaps it's the "friend" who cruelly slandered you. Maybe
it's the spouse who betrayed you. Perhaps it's the person who
sexually, physically, or emotionally abused you. Or, as with Jesus,
perhaps it's a prodigal child who has broken your heart days without end. It's typically easy to lament over *our pain*. But Jesus is
lamenting over *their sin, lostness, and away-ness*. That's other-cen-
tered lament. That's gospel-centered lament.

In John 11:35, Jesus wept over Lazarus. In Luke 19:41, as
Jesus drew near to Jerusalem, "he wept over it." Why the weeping

over a prophet-killing city? Weeping, Jesus said, "Would that you, even you, had known on this day the things that make for peace!" (Luke 19:42). Jesus came to reconcile (to make peace with) the Father's prodigal children. But, like the prodigal of Luke 15, the wayward children of Israel continually chose the broken cisterns of the world over God, the spring of living water. Thus the lament that opens today's devotional: "How often would I have gathered your children together as a hen gathers her brood under her wings, and you were not willing!" (Luke 13:34).

Jesus was not expecting this reconciliation mission to be easy. Have you ever witnessed a hen gathering her brood? It's like herding cats! But Jesus persistently pursues prodigals: "How often would I have gathered your children together . . ."

Once the prodigal returns home, it's easy to care about him or her and to cry tears of joy. But it's not so easy to keep caring and continue ministering when the prodigal keeps resisting our every effort at reconciliation.

Can we be Jesus-like in our pain? Can we lament, weep, care, pray for, and minister to the very ones who break our hearts and cause our grief?

Reflect: Who has deeply hurt you? I've encouraged you to lament and given you permission to grieve many times in our first twentyish days. Today I'm encouraging you to lament for and over *those who have hurt you*. What would your "Psalm of Lament for/over the Grief-Causer" look like today (not a psalm about your loss, but a psalm of compassion over the other person's lostness)?

Reflect: What prayer might God's Spirit be prompting you to pray for the grief-causer in your life (not an "imprecatory" prayer for the demise and defeat of your enemy, but a compassionate prayer for that person to find peace with God)?

DAY 23

Grieving, Yet Giving, by Gripping God

When Jesus knew that his hour had come to depart out of this world to the Father, having loved his own who were in the world, he loved them to the end. (John 13:1)

BIBLICAL WISDOM NEVER suggests that we place ourselves in a position to be re-abused. However, biblical wisdom and Christlike love do teach us what it means to minister to those who have hurt us. In John 13, Jesus, in the grip of grief, grips his Father and gives to his children—even those who will soon abandon him.

Like Jesus, our souls would be troubled if we knew that our time was short (see John 12:27). And, like Jesus, our spirits would be troubled if we knew that a dear friend was going to betray us. "Jesus was troubled in his spirit, and testified, 'Truly, truly, I say to you, one of you will betray me'" (John 13:21).

It is in this context that Jesus "loved them to the end." To the end—of his life! To the end—when Judas betrayed him. To the end—when Peter denied him. To the end—when the crowd chanted, "Crucify him! Crucify him!"

How does Jesus show his endless love to his betrayer and denier? He washes his disciples' feet (see John 13:3–5). Can we serve like that—when our soul is troubled? Can we serve others like that—serving the very ones who are causing our soul's trouble?

Is Jesus the only one who ought to serve his betrayers? He teaches otherwise. "When he had washed their feet and put on his outer garments and resumed his place, he said to them, 'Do you understand what I have done to you? You call me Teacher and Lord, and you are right, for so I am. If I then, your Lord and Teacher, have washed your feet, you also ought to wash one another's feet. For I have given you an example, that you also should do just as I have done to you'" (John 13:12–15).

Do as I have done—in the midst of knowing that my end is near. Do as I have done—to the very one who will expedite my end. Do as I have done—lovingly serving those who are least deserving of your service.

Reading this, I'm sure we're all asking, How could I possibly love like Christ? Maybe we can answer that question by seeing how Christ was able to love like Christ! John tells us: "Jesus, knowing that the Father had given all things into his hands, and that he had come from God and was going back to God," rose from the table to stoop to serve his undeserving disciples (John 13:3).

Do we know, like Jesus, that the Father has given us every good and perfect gift that we need in order to live a godly life? Do we know, like Jesus, that we have come from the Father and are going back to the Father—that our lives are in his trustworthy hands?

We grieve, yet give, by gripping God. Or, better yet, we grieve, yet give, by grasping that God is gripping us.

Reflect: What difficult, or even hurtful, person is Jesus calling you to love with his love? What would wise, biblical truth-in-love look like in this person's life?

Act: Let's be honest: it's not easy to discern what wise love looks like. Perhaps it would be helpful and healthy for you to ask a trusted friend or two for counsel about how to wisely love this person.

DAY 24

Let Not Your Heart Be Troubled

"Let not your hearts be troubled. Believe in God; believe also in me. In my Father's house are many rooms. If it were not so, would I have told you that I go to prepare a place for you? And if I go and prepare a place for you, I will come again and will take you to myself, that where I am you may be also." (John 14:1–3)

JOHN 14:1–3 IS an oft-read New Testament funeral passage. And for good reason. The context is clearly grief—anticipatory grief. The disciples' hearts are troubled because Jesus has shared that he *will be* crucified.

Anticipatory grief is sometimes more disabling than reactionary grief. The loved one receives the diagnosis, and you grieve every hour, every day, day after day, while the illness slowly takes over their body, or mind, or both.

Why shouldn't our hearts be troubled when trouble comes? If this life is all there is, then hopelessness is understandable. So Jesus directs our troubled hearts to a trustworthy God and an untroubled future. Our God not only fearfully and wonderfully makes us but is also fearfully and wonderfully making an eternal home for us—where we will dwell *with Jesus forever*.

Future hope does not obliterate our current pain. It can, however, soothe our pain as we soothe our soul in our Savior's future promise.

Loss often makes us feel like losers, loners, and orphans. "Does anyone care? Can anyone relate? Why me? What's wrong with me?" That's why Jesus does not give us a future promise and then leave us alone. He also gives us a present promise. "I will ask the Father, and he will give you another Helper, to be with you forever, even the Spirit of truth, whom the world cannot receive, because it neither sees him nor knows him. You know him, for he dwells with you and will be in you. I will not leave you as orphans; I will come to you" (John 14:16–18).

Jesus promises that we are *not* orphans. We are not alone. He will be with us and *in* us, *now* and *forever*, by his Spirit.

Loss also causes us to feel turmoil, distress, confusion, and fear. Jesus offers us peace—wholeness, rest, comfort, and courage. It's not the world's false peace of the denial of reality. It's the Word's true peace of eternal reality.

Listen and lean into Jesus's words of peace to you:

> Peace I leave with you; my peace I give to you. . . . Let not your hearts be troubled, neither let them be afraid. (John 14:27)

> I have said these things to you, that in me you may have peace. In the world you will have tribulation. But take heart; I have overcome the world. (John 16:33)

Jesus *never* denies the troubles of this present, dark world. However, he *always* enters our darkness with the light of his presence.

Reflect: When have you experienced anticipatory grief? How has it been almost as difficult as, or perhaps more difficult than, reactionary grief?

Reflect: This week, how could you specifically apply these three promises to your grief journey?

- Anticipatory Hope: "Where I Am You May Be Also"
- Participatory Hope: "I Will Not Leave You As Orphans"
- Participatory Peace: "My Peace I Give to You"

DAY 25

"Man of Sorrows"

Taking with him Peter and the two sons of Zebedee, he began to be sorrowful and troubled. Then he said to them, "My soul is very sorrowful, even to death; remain here, and watch with me." (Matt. 26:37–38)

He took with him Peter and James and John, and began to be greatly distressed and troubled. (Mark 14:33)

TODAY WE DELVE into the suffering Savior's sorrow at Gethsemane. How do his candid lament and deep emotional sorrow impact how we view and express our grief?

God designed us as emotional beings. Emotions, feelings, and moods are God's idea. Therefore they are *not*, in and of themselves, sinful. In fact, they can be beautiful expressions of our creation in God's image. Jesus is a deeply emotional being. His grief in the garden makes that abundantly clear.

Let's ponder together each of these phrases from Matthew and Mark:

- Matthew pulls no punches as he informs us that Jesus was *sorrowful*. The word means to grieve—to be filled with sorrow, emotional heaviness, and deep sadness. Jesus is overflowing with grief. This reminds us of the language of the psalmist in Psalm 42:5–6, where his soul is cast down and he's in turmoil without and within.
- Jesus is *troubled*. He is in anguish; his heart is incredibly heavy; his chest feels crushed emotionally. The KJV translates it as "heavy"—Jesus is heavy-hearted and deeply troubled emotionally.
- In case we are missing the intensity, Matthew uses an intensive form of the word for *grief* in verse 38—Jesus is *very*

sorrowful and deeply grieved. He is overwhelmed emotionally to the point of death. It sounds like a passage from Paul's life that we've explored previously—2 Corinthians 1:8–9, where Paul was utterly burdened beyond his strength so that he despaired of life and felt the sentence of death.

- In Mark 14:33, Mark adds the phrase *greatly distressed*. This Greek word means to be astonished. Jesus is "sore amazed." The word means to feel terror and to be in shock.

If you ever needed scriptural permission to grieve, if you ever needed a biblical reminder that grief is normal, you should find it here in Gethsemane with Jesus. Let the words in the bullet points above sink in. May they be rich reminders that our sinless Savior is a man of sorrows acquainted with grief. Since it is honorable and holy for Jesus to grieve, deeply, it is honorable and holy for you to grieve deeply.

Reflect: As you reread Matthew 26:37–38 and Mark 14:33 along with the four bullet-point descriptions, which word, phrase, or explanation stands out to you? Why? How does it impact you? Resonate with you? In what ways do you identify with Jesus in his grief?

Reflect: In what ways does Jesus's holy grief "free you to grieve"? What will you do differently after having entered and experienced the grief of Jesus?

DAY 26

"Watch with Me"

*And taking with him Peter and the two sons of Zebedee, he began
to be sorrowful and troubled. Then he said to them, "My soul is very
sorrowful, even to death; remain here, and watch with me." . . . And
he came to the disciples and found them sleeping. And he said to Peter,
"So, could you not watch with me one hour?" (Matt. 26:37–38, 40)*

YESTERDAY, DURING DAY 1 of our three days with Jesus
in Gethsemane, we witnessed Jesus modeling holy grief. Today
we will witness him modeling holy need for others. At times, the
Christian world has communicated that emotions and grief are
bad or weak. Jesus dispels that false notion. At other times, the
Christian world has communicated that needing others is bad,
weak, and even sinful. Again, Jesus dispels that false notion.

In the beginning, God created us with a holy need for others. "The LORD God said, 'It is not good that the man should be
alone; I will make him a helper fit for him'" (Gen. 2:18). Unfallen
Adam was in a perfect paradise in perfect relationship with the
perfect God of the universe. Yet God still said that Adam had a
deep need for human companionship.

So it should not seem odd that Jesus took Peter and the two
sons of Zebedee with him into the garden of Gethsemane. Being
human, Jesus stood in need not only of food, drink, clothing,
shelter, and sleep, but also of human fellowship. Jesus needed
these three men. Let that sink in. Jesus needed these three men . . .

"And *taking with him* Peter and the two sons of Zebedee,
he began to be sorrowful." Those three words, *taking with him,*
could be a motto for all grievers. Granted, there are times when
we grieve by ourselves, away from others, in our hearts, just God
and us. Yet those times should and even must be surrounded by

63

grieving with others and *taking others with us*. God did not design us to grieve alone. God designed the body of Christ to grieve together. God calls his people to "rejoice with those who rejoice, weep with those who weep" (Rom. 12:15). "God has so composed the body . . . that the members may have the same care for one another. If one member suffers, all suffer together; if one member is honored, all rejoice together" (1 Cor. 12:24–26).

Jesus models holy disappointment. He asked Peter and the two sons of Zebedee to watch with him. He wanted and needed them to be on emotional sentry duty *with him*. But they went emotionally AWOL. And *it disappointed Jesus*. "He came to the disciples and found them sleeping. And he said to Peter, 'So, could you not watch with me one hour?'" (Matt. 26:40). Can you hear the emotional disappointment? Can you feel the emotional fatigue? Jesus does not lash out, but neither does he minimize or deny the reality that they have let him down.

We have said previously that *shared sorrow is endurable sorrow*. We've painted pictures of *climbing in the grief casket with each other*. Jesus longed for his disciples to climb into his casket of sorrow, but they fell asleep on their watch. And it hurt Jesus.

Reflect: Think about having a *holy need for others*. Who do you need to invite into your casket, to invite on your grief journey?

Reflect: Think about *holy disappointment*. Who has let you down by going off grief sentry duty with you? How could you lovingly express your need for this person to keep watch with you?

DAY 27

"Not My Will but Thine Be Done"

And going a little farther he fell on his face and prayed, saying, "My Father, if it be possible, let this cup pass from me; nevertheless, not as I will, but as you will." . . . Again, for the second time, he went away and prayed, "My Father, if this cannot pass unless I drink it, your will be done." . . . So, leaving them again, he went away and prayed for the third time, saying the same words again. (Matt. 26:39, 42, 44)

WHAT DO WE do when grief emotionally overwhelms us to the point of death? What do we do when others relationally disappoint us by abandoning us in our grief? Today we learn the answer: we cry out to God in holy need for him as our heavenly Father.

When Jesus expressed his sorrow to his disciples, they slumbered and abandoned him. They were so unlike his Father who never slumbers or sleeps, who never leaves us or forsakes us (see Heb. 13:5–6). The disciples could not be there for Jesus even for a few minutes in his darkest hour. What do we do when those who should love us best instead fail us most in our darkest hour? Like Jesus, we should fall on our faces and pray, saying, "My Father who art in heaven . . ." While we need one another, the only one we can count on to be eternally faithful is our heavenly Father.

What does Jesus pray? "My Father, if it be possible, let this cup pass from me . . ." Jesus knew he had come to earth for this very hour, for this very reason, for this very cup (John 12:27–28). Yet he prays, with holy honesty, *"If it be possible . . ."*

Can we be this honest with our desires? "If it be possible, take this grief from me."

Can we be this humble in our submission? "Not my will, but yours be done." In the vortex of his horrible sorrow, in the tsunami of his disciples' abandonment (and betrayal . . . and rejection), we witness our suffering Savior's holy submission to his heavenly Father. "Nevertheless, not as I will, but as you will." "My Father, if this cannot pass unless I drink it, your will be done."

We often follow the false belief that life is either/or: either we are honest with our desires or we reverently submit to God's will. Jesus models the both/and truth:

- *We can be honest with our desires*: "Father, if it is possible, please restore what is lost. Please return my prodigal child. Please reconcile my marriage. Please completely heal me from my past trauma . . ."
- *And we can be humble in our submission*: "But, Father, if this grief cannot pass, if this circumstance cannot change, if my emotions will not be totally healed until heaven, then I submit my will to your wise and loving will. I surrender all."

Reflect: Acknowledge your *holy need for our heavenly Father*—in your grief today, what would it mean to fall on your face before your heavenly Father in holy need?

Act: Practice *holy honesty with our heavenly Father*—pray the desires of your heart. What do you wish were different? Humbly share those wants with your listening Abba, Father.

Act: Practice *holy submission to our heavenly Father*—pray Jesus's prayer of surrender about your grief, loss, and suffering. "Not my will, but yours be done."

DAY 28

"My God, My God, Why Hast Thou Forsaken Me?"

Jesus cried out with a loud voice, saying, "Eli, Eli, lema sabachthani?" that is, "My God, my God, why have you forsaken me?" (Matt. 27:46)

Jesus, calling out with a loud voice, said, "Father, into your hands I commit my spirit!" And having said this he breathed his last. (Luke 23:46)

THE MOST HAUNTING words in all eternity are these: "My God, my God, why have you forsaken me?"

We've come nearly full circle. We began our journey with Jesus being forever one with the Father, in John 1:1. "In the beginning was the Word, and the Word *was with God* . . ." Now we witness the Word *without* God. The Word *forsaken* by God.

How can God forsake God?

How do we respond when we, like Jesus, feel God-forsaken?

How do we respond? We respond like Jesus—with utter, guttural openness. We ask the question that we're afraid to ask, but that Jesus and the psalmists courageously and vulnerably voiced. We respond with the lament of Psalm 13:1–2. "How long, O LORD? Will you forget me forever? How long will you hide your face from me? How long must I take counsel in my soul and have sorrow in my heart all the day?"

In our despair, we lament like the psalmist in Psalm 22:1–2, whom Jesus quotes on the cross. "My God, my God, why have you forsaken me? Why are you so far from saving me, from the words of my groaning? O my God, I cry by day, but you do not answer, and by night, but I find no rest."

In our confusion, we lament like Asaph and his "Psalm of the Dark Night of the Soul" in Psalm 88:15–18. "From my youth I have suffered and been close to death; I have borne your terrors and am in despair. Your wrath has swept over me; your terrors have destroyed me. All day long they surround me like a flood; they have completely engulfed me. You have taken from me friend and neighbor—*darkness is my closest friend*" (NIV).

Our suffering Savior's last words on the cross do not end with God-forsakenness. No—we hear our Savior calling out with a loud voice, "Father, into your hands I commit my spirit!" Only then does he breathe his last breath.

Jesus lived every nanosecond face-to-face with his Father. Theologians call it *coram Deo*: living face-to-face in the presence of God. When Jesus felt God-forsaken, he did not talk behind his Father's back; he talked *to* and *with* his Father. And, when Jesus was ready to go home, he didn't talk about God; he talked *to*, surrendered *to*, and trusted *in* God alone.

The story of the cross does not end with God forsaking God. The cross story ends with God the Son clinging to God the Father and with the Father receiving his Son.

Reflect: Can you bring your grief to your Father *coram Deo*—face-to-face with God—today? Like Jesus, you can grieve *coram Deo* by being honest with God about your feelings of God-forsakenness. What would your lament psalm of God-forsakenness sound like?

Reflect: Your grief story does not have to end with God-forsakenness. It can continue with you clinging to God's trustworthiness. In your pain and despair, what would it mean today for you to say, "Father, into your hands I commit my spirit"?

DAY 29

Your Resurrected Savior
Knows Your Name

Jesus said to her, "Woman, why are you weeping? Whom are you
seeking?" Supposing him to be the gardener, she said to him, "Sir, if
you have carried him away, tell me where you have laid him, and I will
take him away." Jesus said to her, "Mary." She turned and said to him
in Aramaic, "Rabboni!" (which means Teacher). (John 20:15–16)

THE GRAND NARRATIVE of the Bible does not end on the
cross. The Bible's redemptive narrative progresses to the explo-
sive power of Christ's hope-giving resurrection.

Your grief narrative does not end with loss. God's redemptive narrative invades your grief with the promise of resurrection
hope. "We do not want you to be uninformed . . . that you may not
grieve as others do who have no hope. For since we believe that
Jesus died and rose again, even so, through Jesus, God will bring
with him those who have fallen asleep" (1 Thess. 4:13–14). We
grieve, but never as the hopeless ones.

It's one thing to hear about resurrection hope. It's quite
another to personalize it. Mary experienced that as she saw the
empty tomb *and even saw the risen Savior!* However, until she
heard her name, "Mary," she did not believe in him and receive
his resurrection hope.

It's the first day of the week. Mary Magdalene comes to the
tomb so early that it's still dark. Seeing the stone rolled away, she
assumes that someone has taken Jesus out of the tomb. She is
weeping when she turns around and sees Jesus standing outside
the tomb—but she doesn't know it's him.

Jesus asks her, "Woman, why are you weeping? Whom are
you seeking?" (John 20:15). Mary thinks Jesus is the gardener

and wants to know where he's put Jesus! Then "Jesus said to her, 'Mary'" (John 20:16). Not only does Jesus know her name, he calls her by her name: "Mary."

Finally Mary recognizes him, calling him *Rabboni* ("Teacher"). Jesus exhorts Mary not to cling to him—which at first blush might seem confusing. But Jesus doesn't want her clinging to earthly hope. He wants Mary to cling to eternal, heavenly, resurrection hope. "Jesus said to her, 'Do not cling to me, for I have not yet ascended to the Father; but go to my brothers and say to them, 'I am ascending to my Father and your Father, to my God and your God'" (John 20:17).

The Bible's narrative doesn't even end with resurrection hope. It moves to ascension hope—Jesus sovereignly seated on his throne. That's hope. That's the hope we need when our earthly story is replete with defeat. We need to hear our resurrected Savior *and* ascended reigning King reminding us *personally—by name*—that he has ascended to the Father. The same power that paid for our sins, that raised Jesus from the dead, that crushed Satan, and that seated Christ at the right hand of the Father is at work within us who believe (see Eph. 1:15–23). It is transforming our earthly story of grief into an ascension story of victory.

Reflect: Christ's resurrection and ascension are not simply theological doctrines—they are life truths to apply to our life story. What does it mean for you to personalize these doctrines—to hear the resurrected and ascended Savior calling you by name and reminding you personally of your victory in Jesus?

Act: In Ephesians 1:15–23, Paul prays that the saints at Ephesus will have eyes to apply Christ's resurrection and ascension to their life stories. Read Ephesians 1:15–23, praying that the Spirit will open the eyes of your heart to see how Christ's resurrection and ascension impact your grief journey.

DAY 30

The Lens of the Cross

When he was at table with them, he took the bread and
blessed and broke it and gave it to them. And their eyes were
opened, and they recognized him. (Luke 24:30–31)

AS WE NEAR the end of our journey, we sneak a peek at the
road to Emmaus, where two grieving followers of Jesus literally
journeyed with him. Yet they did not recognize him . . . at least
not at first.

Not knowing who they were talking to, they summarized for
Jesus all that had happened from Friday to Sunday. They explained
their hope that Jesus was the one to redeem Israel. Yet the Hope
of Israel was right there with them! What was blinding them?

Jesus tells us. "O foolish ones, and slow of heart to believe
all that the prophets have spoken! Was it not necessary that the
Christ should suffer these things and enter into his glory?" (Luke
24:25–26). These two travelers, the twelve disciples, the crowds
that followed Jesus, the Jewish officials, and the crowd on Passion
Week all wore the same blinders. None of them could compre-
hend a suffering Savior.

In our flesh, we follow a theology of glory. It falsely teaches
that Jesus promises us health and wealth—future glory without
present suffering. This false theology sets us up for disappointment and drives us to despair when loss crashes down on us.

Jesus teaches a theology of the cross. It was necessary that
Christ suffer *before* entering into glory. Moses and all the prophets
predicted this suffering Messiah.

My favorite Bible college professor often said, "If you're in
Christ, you're in him *for the whole experience*. Not just the glory,
but also the suffering." That's the message of Romans 8:16–17.

"The Spirit himself bears witness with our spirit that we are children of God, and if children, then heirs—heirs of God and fellow heirs with Christ, provided we suffer with him in order that we may also be glorified with him."

Suffering is horrible, but the worst suffering comes when we doubt God's goodness because we believe Satan's lie: "God promised only good things for you. Bad things are happening. So you can't trust God!" To counter this lie, we must ground ourselves in God's truth from God's Word about God's Son, our suffering Savior. That's why Jesus "interpreted to them in all the Scriptures the things concerning himself" (Luke 24:27). That's why they said to each other, "Did not our hearts burn within us . . . while he opened to us the Scriptures?" (Luke 24:32). Remember—we live by every word that comes from the mouth of God (see Matt. 4:4).

Theology matters. Truth matters. Applying the Bible's message of a suffering Savior matters in our suffering. Notice when the light dawned for these two disciples: when Jesus took the bread, blessed and broke it, and gave it to them. *Then* "their eyes were opened, and they recognized him" (Luke 24:31). They saw the light *in the breaking of bread*—in that act of communion and remembrance of Christ's blood shed and his body sacrificed for them.

A cross-centered lens is our only hope. We must view and interpret all of life—and especially our suffering—in light of Christ's suffering on our behalf.

Reflect: Interpreting grief means looking at life with cross-centered lenses, as we've done for thirty days. Of every cross-centered lesson in our devotional, which one stands out as the most helpful for you on your grief journey? How? Why?

Reflect: Of all the passages from the Gospels that we've applied to grief, which have been most important for you? Why? How will you continue to apply them?

DAY 31

The Rest of the Story

And while they were gazing into heaven as he went, behold, two men stood by them in white robes, and said, "Men of Galilee, why do you stand looking into heaven? This Jesus, who was taken up from you into heaven, will come in the same way as you saw him go into heaven." (Acts 1:10–11)

GRIEF SHADOWS OUR vision. It so clouds our perspective that we see only the painful past and the empty present. The gospel opens the eyes of our hearts. We see our crucified Savior. Jesus is a suffering Savior who is intimately acquainted with our grief. *It's normal to hurt.* He is a compassionate Savior who lovingly consoles us in our grief. *It's possible to find comfort in our hurt.*

But we don't stop there—we see our resurrected Savior. Jesus is a healing Savior who compassionately speaks eternal truth into our earthly wounds. *It's possible to grieve with hope.*

He is an empowering Savior who mightily enables us to comfort others with the comfort we receive from God. *It's supernatural to love in the midst of loss.*

Peter learns this lesson in John 21, when Jesus invites Peter to come and have breakfast with him. During their meal, Peter receives Jesus's personal commission: *shepherd others!* When your heart breaks, turn to the suffering Shepherd—and, through his comfort and in his strength, comfort and shepherd others also. Do something great for your great Savior *by serving others.*

The gospel also opens our eyes to the ascension and return. That's the rest of the story. When we forget the end of the story, we're tempted to live as if this life were the only story.

The disciples were like that. When they came together after his resurrection, they asked Jesus, "Lord, will you at this time restore the kingdom to Israel?" (Acts 1:6). In other words, "Will

73

you fix us now? Will you fix everything now?" They were willing to settle for temporary recovery. Jesus exhorted them to wait hopefully for the final restoration. And while they wait, like Peter in John 21, they are to do something great. "You will receive power when the Holy Spirit has come upon you, and you will be my witnesses in Jerusalem and in all Judea and Samaria, and to the end of the earth" (Acts 1:8).

But witnessing in the middle of a battlefield can get exhausting, can't it? So we need a final reminder of the end of the story. "Jesus, who was taken up from you into heaven, will come in the same way as you saw him go into heaven" (Acts 1:11).

The end of the story is not crucifixion. It's not even resurrection. Not even ascension. The end of the story is Jesus's return! May this description of the end of your story invade and impact your daily story today. "And I heard a loud voice from the throne saying, 'Behold, the dwelling place of God is with man. He will dwell with them, and they will be his people, and God himself will be with them as their God. He will wipe away every tear from their eyes, and death shall be no more, neither shall there be mourning, nor crying, nor pain anymore, for the former things have passed away'" (Rev. 21:3–4).

Reflect: Do something great! Look upward to Christ and live outward for others. What great act of service to others is God calling you to and empowering you for—even in the midst of your grief?

Reflect: Remember the future! How can remembering that great future day impact your gospel-grief journey with Jesus today?

CONCLUSION

"God of Peace"

"I have said these things to you, that in me you may have peace. In the world you will have tribulation. But take heart; I have overcome the world." (John 16:33)

Take Heart

We began our grief journey by highlighting Jesus as *the man of sorrows*. We commence our growth journey by looking at Jesus, the God-man, who is the *God of peace*.

Jesus is brutally honest: in this world you *will* have trouble. The word *trouble* pictures suffocating pressure from every direction, being squashed, having the breath knocked out of you, having your heart ripped out of your chest—out of your soul.

Jesus is also eternally en*couraging*—placing courage within, stirring up God-given courage. "Take heart." Though our flesh and our heart may fail, God is the strength of our heart. He is the divine heart Surgeon who performs spiritual CPR on our grieving hearts.

The world's "stages" of grief end with "acceptance." You *survive*.

The Word's journey of grief with Jesus doesn't "end"; it commences—it is a new start, a new beginning. And it is not mere "acceptance"—"This is all there is; I have to move on somehow . . ." Through Christ it is much more. You *thrive*—you grow through grieving by grace. "Through the God of peace, I can find shalom—new healing, heart health, and wholeness. And as my broken heart is revived, I am healed to do something great."

Comforting Others with Christ's Comfort

What is that "something great"? It is the "ministry posture" that we learned about in Day 6. The God of all comfort offers us his comfort *so that* we can *comfort others* from the overflow of his infinite comfort (see 2 Cor. 1:3–7).

You are more than a survivor. You are an overcomer, just like Jesus: "But take heart; I have overcome the world" (John 16:33). Your grief is not wasted. God uses your loss and redeems your pain. He heals your broken heart—little by little, day by day in this life, and then totally and forever in heaven. Your healing heart becomes a vessel, God's vessel, for bringing his healing hope and perfect peace to others.

Acknowledgments

I'M THANKFUL FOR my extended family, who walked with me through our most recent family loss—the loss of my brother, Steve, to cancer. I'm especially grateful to my mom, Elaine, as it is beyond words to describe what it is for a mother to lose a son. Mom, your honesty, your candor, your grief—and your hope—all gave me hope. Thank you. I love you, Mom.

And I'm thankful that during this difficult time, God created for us beauty for ashes, as three weeks before Steve's passing he wonderfully surrendered his life to Christ as his Savior. I love you, Lord.

And I'm thankful for the editor of this series, and my friend, Pastor Deepak Reju. "Dee," you have always been such an encourager to me. Thank you for encouraging me to write this devotional—Christ ministered to me as I wrote.

Notes

Tips for Reading This Devotional
1. Jonathan Leeman, *Reverberation: How God's Word Brings Light, Freedom, and Action to His People* (Chicago: Moody, 2011), 19.

Day 11: A Portrait of Gospel Grief with Grace
1. Part of what it means to "love an abuser" biblically is to expose the abuse to those in authority.

Day 15: The Greatest Loss
1. See the following accounts, as described by all three Synoptic Gospels: Matt. 16:21-26; Mark 8:31-37; Luke 9:22-25; Matt. 17:22-23; Mark 9:30-32; Luke 9:43-45; Matt. 20:17-19; Mark 10:32-34; Luke 18:31-34; Matt. 26:1-5; Mark 14:1-2; Luke 21:37-22:2.

Suggested Resources
for the Journey

Guthrie, Nancy. *Holding On to Hope: A Pathway through Suffering to the Heart of God*. Carol Streams, IL: Tyndale Momentum, 2015. [Nancy Guthrie knows what it is to be plunged into life's abyss. Framing her own story of staggering loss and soaring hope with the biblical story of Job, she takes you by the hand and guides you on a pathway through pain, straight to the heart of God.]

Hodges, Samuel J., IV, and Kathy Leonard. *Grieving with Hope: Finding Comfort as You Journey through Loss*. Grand Rapids: Baker Books, 2011. [This book is packed with short, biblically based, gospel-centered, topical chapters addressing the issues that grieving people face but are often hesitant to mention to others.]

Kellemen, Robert W. *God's Healing for Life's Losses: How to Find Hope When You're Hurting*. Winona Lake, IN: BMH Books, 2010. [Are you ready for real, raw, honest, and hopeful conversation about suffering, loss, and grief—from a Christian perspective? When life's losses invade your world, learn how to face suffering face-to-face with God through *God's Healing for Life's Losses*.]

Viars, Stephen. *Putting Your Past in Its Place: Moving Forward in Freedom and Forgiveness*. Eugene, OR: Harvest House, 2011. [For those who are grieving over sin and suffering, Pastor Steve Viars provides practical, biblical answers for understanding the important place that Scripture gives to the past, for replacing guilt and despair with forgiveness and hope, and for turning failures into stepping stones for growth.]

BIBLICAL
COUNSELING
COALITION

The Biblical Counseling Coalition (BCC) is passionate about enhancing and advancing biblical counseling globally. We accomplish this through broadcasting, connecting, and collaborating.

Broadcasting promotes gospel-centered biblical counseling ministries and resources to bring hope and healing to hurting people around the world. We promote biblical counseling in a number of ways: through our *15:14* podcast, website (biblicalcounselingcoalition.org), partner ministry, conference attendance, and personal relationships.

Connecting biblical counselors and biblical counseling ministries is a central component of the BCC. The BCC was founded by leaders in the biblical counseling movement who saw the need for and the power behind building a strong global network of biblical counselors. We introduce individuals and ministries to one another to establish gospel-centered relationships.

Collaboration is the natural outgrowth of our connecting efforts. We truly believe that biblical counselors and ministries can accomplish more by working together. The BCC Confessional Statement, which is a clear and comprehensive definition of biblical counseling, was created through the cooperative effort of over thirty leading biblical counselors. The BCC has also published a three-part series of multi-contributor works that bring theological wisdom and practical expertise to pastors, church leaders, counseling practitioners, and students. Each year we are able to facilitate the production of numerous resources, including books, articles, videos, audio resources, and a host of other helps for biblical counselors. Working together allows us to provide robust resources and develop best practices in biblical counseling so that we can hone the ministry of soul care in the church.

To learn more about the BCC, visit biblicalcounselingcoalition.org.

More Counseling Resources by Bob Kellemen

Bob Kellemen proves that we can have victory when anxiety strikes and even learn how to use it. In this biblical study, he lays out a proper Christian view of anxiety, from creation to fall to redemption to consummation. Along the way, he helps us to apply the gospel to our daily lives and reclaim anxiety for what it should be: *vigilance* to motivate us to do God's work.

Can the church truly help those who have been sexually abused? Bob Kellemen says yes, it can. He realistically portrays the damages wrought by sexual abuse and the relevancy of God's Word to this difficult topic. He then takes us on a journey toward healing, helping sufferers to reclaim beauty from the ashes of abuse and to move from being victims to victors.

The Gospel for Real Life booklet series by the Association of Biblical Counselors (ABC) applies the timeless hope of Christ to the unique struggles of modern believers.

More Resources by Bob Kellemen

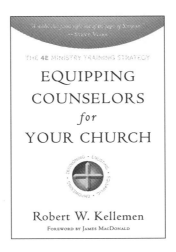

Want to change lives? Here is a best-practice tool for empowering God's people to make disciples. Launch a revolution in one-another disciple-making, and equip your church to become a place not simply *with* biblical counseling, but *of* biblical counseling.

"Bob Kellemen . . . wants to see your church's one-on-one ministry transformed. The way he does that is by giving clear, practical instruction along with a huge package of supplies and tools."
—**Edward Welch**, counselor and faculty member, Christian Counseling and Educational Foundation; author, *When People Are Big and God Is Small*

"An excellent resource for both individual leaders and also group discussion. This is the book for you if you want to launch a biblical counseling ministry."
—**Randy Patten**, former executive director, National Association of Nouthetic Counselors